A Longworth Story

A Stonemason and his family

Jan Kelly 2013

Contents

Foreword

This is the story of twentieth century Longworth as seen through the lives of one man and his family during an amazing period of war, upheaval and social change. This man is in many ways the 'Everyman' of his day: he represents the ordinary family man living through extraordinarily difficult and often dreadful times. Who could guess when seeing Longworth today, a hugely attractive and peaceful backwater, that such lives could have been lived here in recent times?

Harry and Flo Mansell, born towards the close of the Victorian era, were Mary Mansell's parents-in-law. This book is dedicated to Mary and her son Harry Edward Reginald Mansell, formerly of Little Owls, Lodge Lane, Longworth. Without Mary and her patience, kindness, constant availability and willingness to answer countless questions, this book would still be in the form of a heap of memorabilia lying in various archive boxes! Mary never met her father-in-law and Harry never met his grandson young Harry who, now in his mid-thirties, will never know his family's or his village's history.

As Mary Mansell, the last member of the Mansell family to live in Longworth, prepared to leave the district in the summer of 2009 she gave her family archive – drawers full of family albums, old letters, coupons, ration books, wartime letters, receipts for old cars, architect's plans for houses lived in and many other items – to the Longworth & District History Society for safe-keeping.

Many of us keep family pictures, papers and old bygones but few of us get round to putting them into a coherent story for the family or a wider audience and fewer still let the local History Society have the safe-keeping of them. What with moving house, the vicissitudes of family life and the advent of email and Facebook, our busier life styles and the 'declutter' bug, many of us keep fewer and fewer old paper records. Thank goodness members of the Mansell family hoarded and protected family paperwork going right back before the First World War. Thank goodness Stan Gutteridge and his late brother Tony, whose mother was Flo Mansell's youngest sister, had such detailed memories of the 1930s and 1940s. Priceless!

Writing a local history of a place where the author never lived and where names and events are remembered differently by people whose families have lived there for generations is fraught with potential for misunderstanding. Names of roads changed over time. Houses in small villages rarely had names or street numbers until well after the Second World War but youngsters often gave names to places for their own use. Family 'given' names are repeated generation after generation, and the names are often abbreviated – Florence becomes known as Flo by the family and Florrie by a few others.

Whether someone is remembered as a young boy or as an old man also changes the story and memories can be quirky things. Different generations remember details which are not for disclosure to complete strangers - and this affects the truth. Any mistakes in what follows are my own. I've tried hard to sort out the truth and been mindful of later generations. Tracking down the ownership of photographs and validating the text has been time-consuming but important. If I have missed anyone please get in touch.

Jan Kelly (April 2013)

1. A Stonesfield Slater

In the beginning – North Leigh

Harry Mansell's background was 'set in stone' – literally. Harry Mansell was born to a family of masons and Stonesfield slaters and plasterers in North Leigh, a small village about three miles north-east of Witney in Oxfordshire, on 8th February 1889. The village of North Leigh, where Harry lived for the first 24 years of his life, lies in west Oxfordshire on the south-eastern flanks of the Cotswolds - a beautiful area which at the end of the nineteenth century was a land of peaceful stone villages, like old Berkshire around Longworth. There were many large classical estates such as Blenheim, Wilcote, Ditchley and Cornbury.

North Leigh had many old stone cottages and was less than four miles from Stonesfield and the large quarries (or 'mines', as they were known locally) of Stonesfield 'slate' created when blocks of oolitic limestone (of Jurassic age – like the dinosaurs!) were extracted and then left in fields for the frost to split them. The 'slate mines' produced fine lightweight regular tiles widely used throughout the Cotswolds and much further afield for roofing. Stonesfield slate was (and still is) much sought after, though the mines are now no longer producing new slates and have been designated a 'Site of Special Scientific Interest' looked after by Natural England.

The coming of the railway in 1861 linking Oxford and Witney to Worcester, and the villages in between, had brought new opportunities for the import of red clay tiles, Welsh slate and (later) reconstituted tiles – all of which were lighter too - and so Stonesfield slate slowly began to lose ground as the roof tile of choice.

Map to show the location of the principal villages which feature in the text.

North Leigh and Stonesfield lie on the south-east flank of the Cotswolds.

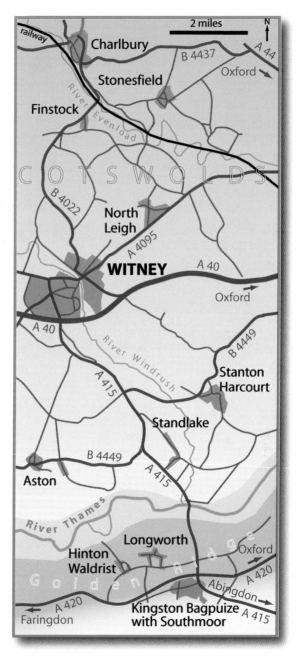

Longworth, once Berkshire but now part of Oxfordshire, lies astride the ridge of hard limestone known as the Golden Ridge.

This local material was relatively expensive despite not having the added expense of long distance carriage by train and was not in keeping with the new brick-built housing which started to spread tentacle-like from many towns and villages in late Victorian times. Stonemasons would gradually give way to general builders, as fewer and fewer buildings were built in stone rather than in the new mass-produced brick or 'phoney-stone', but it was a gradual process. The old stone villages would keep stonemasons going for many years yet.

Building a career

Harry was the third son and seventh child of Leonard and Amenda Mansell. In the opening years of the twentieth century Harry's father (and his father before him) and two of Harry's brothers, Albert and Frederick, were all builder's plasterers – who became journeymen working under a master craftsman. Ivo, the youngest, was a builder's labourer. Harry would have had very little opportunity to choose any other occupation than work in the building trade. It was relatively easy for young men to pick up their father's trade by 'helping out' when they were young. The Mansells had close family connections in the same village – uncles, brothers, cousins and nephews all in the building trade. The proximity to Stonesfield enabled Harry to gain experience in roof tiling from an early age, maybe actually working in the 'slate mines' for a while and he generally described himself as a plasterer/Stonesfield slater. He would eventually become a master builder in these crafts.

Harry, having learned the basics, was apprenticed to a firm in Witney. Apprenticeships dated back to the twelfth century and were a proven way for young men to learn on the job and then have the ability to earn more than just a jobbing builder or builder's mason. By all accounts Harry became an excellent craftsman and was a member of the National Association of Plasterers. Harry was indeed rather lucky to be able to start an apprenticeship.

Amenda Berry (above), first wife of Leonard Mansell (right).

In 1898 when Harry was only nine his mother, Amenda, had sadly died. Harry's eldest sister Emily, twelve years his senior, became housekeeper to the family of younger children still at home - five were under the age of 11.

Even with several of Leonard Mansell's brothers and sisters and older children on hand living in the village, for a working man such as Leonard to lose a wife when there were so many children to feed and care for would have been a bitter blow – sadly not one that was unusual at the time. The eldest daughter Emily would be keen to leave home and lead her own family life and everyone would have been heartily relieved when Leonard married Fanny, his second wife, in 1905 when Harry was 16. By 1911, when Leonard Mansell was approaching 60, the pressure was off as only the two youngest sons, Harry aged 22 and Ivo 17, still lived 'at home' with Leonard and Fanny.

Harry worked for Bartlett Brothers in Witney where he had completed his apprenticeship. This was the leading building firm in the Witney area and employed some of Harry's relatives too. The firm had been established in 1852 by Malachi Bartlett and had their works at 75 High Street in Witney. They worked in brick, stone and wood - making their own bricks and burning their own lime for mortar. They were reputed to have the first steam-driven saw mill and machine shop in the area and by 1880 already used mechanical concrete mixers. The firm had been responsible for building many fine stone buildings in Witney and the surrounding area including the Witney Corn Exchange and the old Police Station on Church Green. Stone (especially Bath stone) was brought in first by road and then by rail; the firm also exported large quantities of local stone and other materials through Witney and Faringdon railway stations.

In 1913 Harry went up to the Liverpool Exhibition which show-cased industrial development and demonstrated the work of 'skilled craftsmen and artificers'. A reproduction of the city of Chester, complete with individual shops, was built to demonstrate the coming

A team of demonstrators at the 1913 Liverpool Exhibition. Harry Mansell is in the back row, fifth from the right and wearing a white 'overall'.

together of the individual trades. Harry worked for the duration of the exhibition in the Palace of Applied Arts and Crafts. His employers chose him and a small group of his fellow workmen to demonstrate their plastering and cornicing skills so they must have been of a high order. It also seems that Harry's brothers, Fred, Albert and Ivo, also went along with him.

Harry's brother, Fred (right), stayed on to work permanently in Liverpool and spent most of his working life there. Fred had worked for a short while as a butler at Chatsworth House in Derbyshire but eventually turned back to building work. Harry, Albert and Ivo returned to Oxfordshire after the Exhibition ended.

The staple work of stonemasons and related trades in rural regions would be maintaining the stock of local houses, farm buildings and shops and working on new houses built in the area. In towns like Witney the larger firms, like Bartlett Bros, would be responsible for the more prestigious and costly buildings and provide opportunities to work with the best stone as well as providing bread-and-butter work.

Harry's skill would have been in high demand. To work for a large firm like that of Bartlett Bros would have been considered a really good job and enabled skilled men to get out into the surrounding catchment area where occasionally extra teams of builders would be called in on certain jobs.

Jesse Richings, stone-mason of Longworth, with his son Will, a mason's labourer, must have worked on building sites where Harry worked and so it was perhaps not surprising that Harry eventually met Jesse's eldest daughter Florence Jane Richings (Flo), just a few weeks after returning from the Liverpool Exhibition.

Florence Jane Richings

10

2. The Stonemason's Family

Central Longworth from the air in the early 1950s. Home Farm is in the foreground (see also the book cover). The Square is in the middle distance.

Flo Richings' family

Flo's home background was also 'set in stone'. Longworth in the early 1900s was a rural backwater of stone cottages with their mix of Stonesfield slate or thatched roofs. Some, but by no means all, of the cottages were small, poorly maintained and overcrowded. There were several families by the name of Richings in Longworth – including those at *Warren Cottage* (all italicised names are shown on the map on the inside back cover) living in Lodge Lane; in The Square; in Richings Row (where Rodney Terrace now stands); at *Sudbury Farmhouse* (a rather larger home) and at *Laburnum Cottage* at the junction of Hinton Road and Cow Lane.

11

The families were all directly or indirectly related to each other and all but one of the Richings' house-holders at this time were men who earned their living as stonemasons and plasterers and had sons who were following on in the masonry trade, and had done for many generations.

Flo's father, Jesse Richings, and his youngest brother Albert worked in partnership together. They lived at *Laburnum Cottage* and used the site of 'Blenheim Cottage' opposite their home, now long since demolished, as a builder's yard. This old cottage had to be demolished, in part, because the well there had 'died' and it had to be filled in.

Laburnum Cottage at the junction between Cow Lane and the Hinton - Appleton Road.

Jesse and Albert lived with their two sisters Agnes and Eliza. Albert was known in the family as 'Uncle Put' - a dab hand with putty and apparently he used masses of it!

When Jesse Richings married his near neighbour Eliza Jane Heath on 31st August 1891, Eliza Jane was living with her mother, Elizabeth, and sister Florence (Flo) in a

12

semi-detached stone and tile cottage on the Hinton Road about 200 yards from where he was brought up. Her late father Albert had worked as a thatcher and was hence allocated a tied cottage on the farm where he worked. It was close to an un-metalled path, known locally as Ham Road leading south to the Faringdon Road - an old turnpike.

Jesse, on marriage, left his childhood home and moved in with Eliza Jane and her mother to await a vacancy in a rented property. Fortunately they were soon able to move next door into the other half of the semi-detached cottage (nearest Ham Road) and over the next eleven years had a family of seven children.

Hinton Road, looking east from the end of Butts Lane. Squirrel Cottage is seen on the immediate right beyond which is Wickham with the turning down Ham Road just beyond that. In the far distance is Laburnum Cottage. Mrs Free, with her bicycle, is on a delivery run from the store and post office in the Square.

Jesse and Eliza Jane's first child, Florence Jane Richings, was born in 1892. She was named after her Aunt Florence and her mother. Tragically their fifth child, Harry Richings, died in 1899 of diphtheria when only seven months old, and their second child Lilian May aged 17 also died of diphtheria in 1911. This illness was no respecter of age! Longworth at the end of the nineteenth century, like most other villages and towns, had successive waves of measles, diphtheria, typhus, whooping cough and other diseases which often proved fatal, especially to young children. At the time of her sister Lilian's early death Flo Richings, aged 18, was living in at the Rectory working as a kitchen-maid - as her mother's sister (Flo senior) had also done - for the Rector and his wife. It would prove to be a good place to work.

"dear Flo
Just a line to let you
know we have got
Poor Barbara down
with whooping cough.
She has had it for a fortnight
Got to sleep downstairs
rather a nuisance Xmas
so near. Evelyn cant
come near us with
babies. So it will be a
poor Xmas. Hope you
are all quite well
so goodbye from your
sister Ida"

14

Young Flo's Longworth

The village where Harry Mansell's future wife, Flo, grew up was a very different place from the Longworth we know today. The centrally-heated, old stone cottages clustered together in a quiet rural village today carry a healthy financial premium. They have benefitted from large sums of money spent converting them into large comfortable family homes. But before the 1960s they were tiny, cold, damp, inconvenient and mostly rented from landlords without the means or the will to keep them waterproof, as well as too far from centres of regular, varied and well-paid employment. Ninety per cent of the workers in Longworth worked on the local farms for very low agricultural wages. The only transport was via carrier and leaving the village for any reason was a big event for most people, certainly before the First World War.

When the new Rector, John Illingworth, and his wife Agnes Louisa (Nora) moved into Longworth Rectory in 1883 they were faced with a community where a great deal needed to be done to improve the lot of many poor families. Much of the welfare, entertainment and social benefits in Longworth, as elsewhere, emanated from the Parish Church or from local chapels and the richer families of the village. Although Jesse Richings' family was by no means poor by contemporary standards, they lived among families that had to work hard, like themselves, to make ends meet. There were so many things which could go wrong – bad weather, wage-earners could be laid off work, family ill health, or the death of the main wage-earner or principal carer. There was no large town close by to give greater opportunities for work or improvement if they were unable to find local work or were not fit for hard, outdoor, all weather, farm work or stonemasonry.

The Rev. John and Nora Illingworth taking tea in the garden of the Rectory in Longworth.

But the new Rector, a highly spiritual man, spent as little time on parochial matters outside his immediate church commitments as was possible. Though aware of the needs of his parish, he was said to abhor clerical meetings and Diocesan affairs and concentrated instead on the more academic aspects of spiritual matters - sermons, services, writing and meetings with like-minded people. Notably, he contributed to the book of essays  called Lux Mundi, which was put together, mainly at the Rectory in Longworth, in long sessions with other highly academic men of religion. This was not a promising scenario for anyone thinking that the new incumbent at the church might, hand in hand with the local chapels, alleviate the desperate conditions faced from time to time by many parishioners in Longworth in late Victorian Longworth.

16

But John Illingworth had a wife – an indomitable lady, an ideal partner, who set about changing the woeful state of the church's finances and enabled it to do a great deal for Longworth's poor.

Nora Illingworth, with her husband focussed on more esoteric matters, revelled in her parish work and with no children to consider she had free rein to do more or less what she wanted. Her husband took an interest of course but left her to do her good works. She increased the financial standing of the church – ensuring the local big houses were informed and fully involved, she changed collections from monthly to weekly; much of the fabric of the church and the pews and other furniture were replaced over time and the church became a friendlier place. The church and the Rectory became the hub of highly practical good works.

Letting the village know what was going on through her regular monthly entries in the church magazine, Nora and her network of relatively wealthy influential friends, including Mr and Mrs Crum at Longworth Manor Farm and Sir Clarendon Golding Hyde and his wife Lady Margery Laura Hyde at Longworth House on Lodge Lane, set up a system of subscription-giving which enabled them to make a very real difference in the parish.

17

They gave practical help to families coping with poverty and needing to earn extra money. Indeed, she employed Flo Mansell, and earlier her Aunt Flo, as domestics at the Rectory and gave them enormous support in preparation for their future lives as wives and mothers. Although several of the Richings family were known to be staunch chapel-goers - including Eliza Jane Richings and at least one of her sons, Will - they nevertheless joined in events and classes offered by the church.

The entry in the England Census of 1911 relating to those occupying Longworth Manor

	1.	2.	3.	4.	6.	10.
1	S. John Richardson Shipworth	Head	62		married	Clergyman. Est. Church g
2	Agnes Louisa Shipworth	Wife		50	married	
3	Helen Maria Cunliffe	Visitor		48	single	
4	Sarah Ann Pyman	Visitor		30	single	
5	Sarah Brooks	Servant		26	single	Cook. (Domestic) 781
6	Mary Collier	Servant		22	single	Housemaid (Domestic)
7	Florence Jane Richings	Servant		18	single	Kitchenmaid (Domestic)
8						

18

In Longworth 'morality', as perceived by those such as Nora Illingworth, as elsewhere, was low – it was quite normal for couples to marry only after the birth of their first or even second or third child. It was a close friend of John and Nora Illingworth who paid for the building of two new red-brick cottages, some of the first in the village, at the top of Lodge Lane to house a parish nurse and the church organist. Mothers' meetings became more focussed and a Mothers' Union was started. Nora saw to it that vaccinations for smallpox were provided as in 1902 there were cases only eight or nine miles away. Membership of the church mushroomed. On Easter Day 1911 there were 73 people who took communion in Longworth Church – for such a chapel-loving village this was an enormous number.

Before John and Nora Illingworth came to the village the only regular clubs or societies in the village were the Coal and Clothing Club and the Sunday School. Now Nora had the Rectory Barn refurbished and re-floored by carpenter Bart Painton of Butts Lane. This provided a central place for the village to come together for concerts, dances, hand-bell practice and Morris dancing (all of which Flo, her sisters and her aunt are known to have enjoyed). There were also plays and other entertainments, school treats, miniature rifle club and lantern slides of the coronation in 1911.

Even political meetings were viewed as entertainment and drew large crowds in Longworth and surrounding villages. Jasmine Howse wrote, 'When there was time for merry-making the Rectory Barn filled the place of a village hall, and a man with a barrel organ came to play for two pence a night. There was a flourishing cricket club, which has since disappeared, and among the rules one was prominently displayed which forbade members to bring beer on to the pitch.'

Mr and Mrs Crum of Longworth Manor brought scouting to the village – the scouts met in the Manor Barn and enjoyed outings and camping in the Manor fields. They were also, apparently, responsible for a major 'soakaway' system which predated Longworth's mains sewage system and which drained down to the withy beds close to Faringdon Road. This would have contributed to improving the health of many in the village when some of the cottage cesspools, which required regular emptying, were no longer required.

Longworth Manor Farm, as it was called in 1906, when owned by Guy Weaving. Three Weaving sisters can be seen sitting on the front steps.

Longworth Manor circa 1911, after the Crum family purchase. Jesse and Albert Richings are building the extension seen above.

Longworth Manor in November 2012.

At about the same time (circa 1911) the Richings were also reponsible for building the Gazebo which graces the north-east corner of the Manor gardens. It abuts an older wall pierced by a four-centred moulded arch over a doorway which allows private access to the church from the manor. Intriguingly, a stone set within this older wall is carved with the initials JR 1791.

The gazebo has a roof of thin beds of limestone flags known as Stonesfield Slates.

The Rectory in 1911.
Flo Heath and Flo Richings worked here.

Poor families were given practical advice and opportunities to improve themselves and get through the more difficult winter season. More money than ever before was donated by the richer families of the community and by regular subscriptions collected from church-goers.

Local landowners and business people such as John Edward Church of Home Farm, Mr Hissey of Roadside Farm (now Fallowfields), Mr Jesse Broughton of the shop (now a house called Hill View) next to Martens Hall, Mr Godfrey of Longworth village, Mrs Weaving of Southmoor, Mrs Bouverie-Pusey of Pusey Manor, rose-grower Mr Alfred Prince of Tuck's Lane and Mr and Mrs W.G. Crum of Longworth Manor, among others in the community, were all listed as regular subscribers. Many other families were supported by their different chapels.

Interestingly, Mrs Illingworth, never one to overlook an interesting new idea when trying to improve the lot of the villagers, wrote,

"We are anxious to get people in Longworth to adopt Lancashire clogs for their children's footwear, and indeed for their own. They outlast several pairs of those usually worn and keep feet warm and dry. For the present they may be ordered in any sizes from the Rectory. If the demand is sufficient we hope to get one of the village shops to stock them. They are no more expensive than ordinary shoes."

History does not record whether many families took heed of the exhortation to wear Lancashire clogs and certainly none of the local children were ever photographed wearing them!

Later it would be the Parish and District Councils which took on many of the roles of the church, chapel and richer families. Jesse Richings, like many a tradesman or businessman did his bit for the community. He had attended the very first Longworth Parish Council Meeting in December 1894. Though Jesse put his name forward for election as a councillor he did not receive quite enough votes.

Those elected were John Edward Church (Jesse's landlord, a gentleman farmer at Home Farm), Henry Albert Brooks (blacksmith of Tuck's Lane), Jesse Broughton (grocer and coal dealer), William Dewe (gentleman of Martens Hall), George Painton (farm labourer of Rose Cottage in High Street), Ernest Richings (farmer at Sudbury Farm) and Jesse Webb (farmer at Draycott Moor).

S. Mary's, Longworth, Parish Magazine.

DECEMBER, 1889.

Holy Communion—1st, after Matins ; all other Sundays at 8-o a.m.
Daily—Matins, 10-0 ; Evensong, 5-0.
Christmas Day—Holy Communion, Matins, Evensong.

Parish Notices.

Snowdrop and the Seven Wee Men.—We regret to say that the performance of this little play must unavoidably be postponed until the warmer weather in the Spring comes.

Coal Club.—The tickets of the Coal and Clothing Clubs were as usual given out the first week in November. The 21 members of the Coal Club paid in £14 14s. 8d., and received £3 3s. as bonus, being 3s. to each member.

Clothing Club.—The 33 members of this Club paid in £22 10s. 8d., and received a bonus of £4 17s. 0d., being 3s. to nearly each person. The subscribers to the two Clubs were : Mr. S. E. Bouverie Pusey, Mrs. E. Powell, Mrs. and Miss Floyd, Mrs. Church, Mrs. Tyrell Brookes, Mrs. John Edmonds, Mrs. C. W. Edmonds, Mrs. Poole, Mrs. T. Duffield.

Children's Christmas Treat.—Subscriptions either in money or kind are requested towards this this month, and will be announced in next month's Magazine. The subscriptions provide prizes in the form of books, and presents of useful clothing, toys, oranges, &c., to each child who has made the required number of attendances. Will anyone give us a TREE for the children this year ?

To Girls in Service.—Mrs. Illingworth wishes to make it known that she will give to any of the girls who have belonged to her class, now in service, stuff for a print gown when they have been in one place a year ; and a wool one when they have been two years, and each year afterwards, or books if they prefer them. She particularly wishes them to apply to her for these gowns or books, but they must in all cases enclose a statement from their mistresses that they have been with them so long, and behaved satisfactorily. It would be a very good thing if all our Longworth girls in service would take in this Magazine. It would only cost them 1/6 a year, and they would see all that was going on in the old home. If they want them they must please order them *at once*.

Christmas Presents.—Will anyone who wishes to give any of the following articles as Christmas presents please order them of Mrs. Illingworth, Longworth Rectory. Faringdon. The proceeds will go towards a new Altar ; and anyone who has seen the Holy Table uncovered will certainly acknowledge that a new one is required :—

	S.	D.
Baby's Warm, Knitted, Wool Bonnets	2	3
,, ,, Caps	1	9
Tam O'Shanters ...from	2	0
Knitted Wool Petticoats ...from	7	6
Bed-room Slippers, Embroidered Silk, without heels, from (according to quality of soles) ...3s. 6d. to	5	0
Nautilus Work Bags, Liberty Cretonnes	2	6

When Harry met Flo

How Harry Mansell and Florence Jane Richings came to meet is, at this remove, very uncertain, but those in the building trades based within 15 miles or so of each other may well have met up on larger building projects. Or perhaps Flo's brother Will, a mason's labourer and plasterer, aged about 17 who became a good friend of Harry's, went up to the 1913 Liverpool Exhibition with Harry in that year.

Having decided not to stay on in Liverpool, as his brother Fred did, and make a career there, Harry returned and later became a regular visitor at the Richings' family home. Country people were usually naturally very friendly and there were obviously no obstacles to the friendship between Harry Mansell and Flo – the eldest daughter of Jesse and Eliza Jane Richings. They would have had so much in common in their backgrounds including an upbringing in a rural village and fathers with similar trades.

Harry and Flo were married on 7th November 1914 just three months after the start of the 'Great War' when Harry was 24 and Flo 22 years old. They were married by the Rev. John Illingworth at Longworth Church.

The marriage was witnessed by Flo's brother Will and sister Agnes and after a wedding breakfast at Flo's home in Hinton Road the two newly-weds set off for their first home together in a cottage at North Leigh close to Harry's parents and his workplace.

*Wedding guests of Harry Mansell and
Florence Jane Richings - November 1914.*

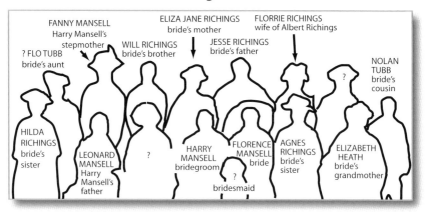

FANNY MANSELL
Harry Mansell's
stepmother

ELIZA JANE RICHINGS
bride's mother

FLORRIE RICHINGS
wife of Albert Richings

? FLO TUBB
bride's aunt

WILL RICHINGS
bride's brother

JESSE RICHINGS
bride's father

NOLAN
TUBB
bride's
cousin

?

HILDA
RICHINGS
bride's
sister

LEONARD
MANSELL
Harry
Mansell's
father

?

HARRY
MANSELL
bridegroom

FLORENCE
MANSELL
bride

?
bridesmaid

AGNES
RICHINGS
bride's
sister

ELIZABETH
HEATH
bride's
grandmother

Hinton Road Cottages

There were two pairs of semi-detached cottages on
Hinton Road not far from the turning into Butts Lane (see
map of Longworth on the inside back cover) and opposite
the pasture land in front of Home Farm which belonged
to the Home Farm estate of John Edward Church. They
were tied cottages where the head of the household
would normally be expected to work on Home Farm land

26

which stretched immediately north and south of the cottages and into other parts of Longworth. Generations of large families were born and brought up in these cottages. In the early part of the twentieth century few people gave their houses a name or number – especially those living in small cottages such as these. Any post would be addressed to the named individual or family, followed occasionally by the name of the road, and then the village name.

Everyone knew everyone else then – including the postman who walked (or later cycled) over from Faringdon. The pair of cottages leased to the Heaths and Richings became referred to by some of a later generation as Wickham Cottages (after local field names) or as 'Lukers' when a family of that name lived there, and the semi-detached cottages next door were much later knocked into one cottage called Squirrel Cottage. But the census enumerator merely referred to them as 'Hinton Road cottages' or 'Church's cottages' after the landlord John Edward Church. Either way, they were easily identifiable.

Jesse and Eliza Jane Richings lived in the east half of the semi next to Ham Road with their children. They lived in this tied cottage despite the head of the household not working on the farm – there must have been no demand for more farmworkers at the time or they would not have been able to rent the cottage. Their cottage was the larger of the two semis – with three rooms downstairs and four rooms upstairs but, as with all the other stone cottages in the Longworth area, they had no inside sanitation or running water. The two semi-detached households shared a well, and a long pole for operating the bucket, with Squirrel Cottage - the thatched pair next door.

Squirrel Cottage 1934

Behind each household at the furthest possible point from the well and the back doors of the cottages was a privy – a 'bucket toilet' behind a hedge of laurel which kept away the flies. The tin roof meant that the privies were hot in summer and cold in winter and noisy whenever it rained. Inside under a wooden seat there was one (or more) galvanised buckets, depending on how many holes were cut into the seat, and which would be emptied onto the small allotment area close by. Each family would organise the weekly emptying of the privy and spread the contents in a trench. Longworth would not have mains sewerage until 1965.

The Heath's next door

In the western half of Wickham Cottages at the time of the 1901 census was Eliza Jane Richings' mother, Elizabeth Heath (see group photo on page 26), who had a right of tenancy as a widow of Albert Heath an erstwhile Home Farm worker. She had brought up two daughters, Eliza Jane and Florence. In 1901, in her sixties, she was living with her four-year-old grandson Frederick Bart Heath. Fred's mother, Florence Heath (known as Flo), was at this time 'living in' at Longworth Rectory. In 1897 at the age of twenty-two and unmarried she had given birth to Fred. Being born out of wedlock could have been a poisoned chalice, but as William the Conqueror, Queen Elizabeth I and Sir Alec Guinness (among many others) might have attested, it was not always the case. Despite a certain amount of gossip and speculation about the likely father, most Longworth residents, including the child himself, would have taken a very relaxed attitude and there always seemed to be someone available in the large extended families of the day to bring up an extra child - especially one as prepossessing as Fred - he won prizes at Sunday School and became an accomplished musician.

Single mother Flo Heath needed to earn a living – she had no father alive to support her and no old-age pension or other welfare benefits for her mother or her son. Elizabeth Heath looked after her grandson whilst Flo was a servant at Longworth Rectory. Flo worked at the Rectory with two others, a cook, Annie Rulties, and a between-maid Fanny Eldridge.

Nora Illingworth was well-known for trying to help the young women of the parish by finding them employment where possible and using various strategies to improve their morals and provide them with craft skills such as lace-making to enable them to earn extra cash after children came along.

Flo Heath (later Mrs Tubb) outside her home in Church Road (circa 1939)

Flo Heath was not only given employment as their own live-in servant at a time when she needed financial support but she was also encouraged to make very high quality lace to provide further income. So talented was Flo that a piece of her gold torchon lace was chosen in 1908 by Queen Alexandra who bought it from among samples sent to Buckingham Palace by the Kingston Bagpuize and Longworth Lace Industry which had begun under the auspices of Mrs Illingworth and her close friend Mrs Lessing, the sister of Edward Strauss at Kingston House.

Family wedding photographs testify to the pride shown in the wearing of lace collars by the ladies. Flo Heath's young niece Flo Richings also gained credit for the quality of her lace. On Bank Holiday Monday in 1906 Flo (junior) aged 14 won a prize for her lace pillow shown at Kingston Bagpuize Flower Show. Both aunt and niece had attended the lace and plain sewing classes run by Mrs Cadnam, the tutor paid for by Nora Illingworth and Mrs Lessing. Lace and other items were advertised for sale locally or even as far afield as London and Birmingham and brought in much-needed extra cash.

With Flo Heath's only sibling (Eliza Jane) living next door with her husband Jesse and growing family, her mother Elizabeth had plenty of room (by late nineteenth century standards) in her cottage to bring up a grandson. Fred Heath turned out to be an exceptional man and an exceptional musician – playing the church organ to great effect. On leaving the village school he worked as an assistant at the 'butter factory' in Hinton Waldrist. His employer George Batts had set up a profitable side-line to his carrier's business and his farming with his brother Albert and established this small unit at the side of his home in the main street. Fred helped to wash and blend large blocks of Irish butter and re-packaged them

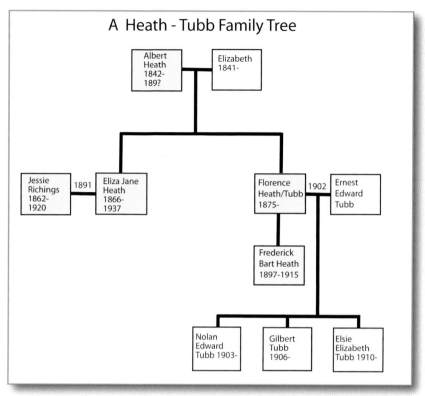

A Heath - Tubb Family Tree

aesthetically to add value to the product. Then George and Albert would distribute the butter locally and to towns and villages in the area. But, tragically, the young butter-maker Fred Heath was to die very young.

In 1902 Flo Heath married Ernest Edward Tubb (known to many as Lazzy) an agricultural worker on Home Farm and Sunday school teacher at Longworth Church. He was living in a rundown cottage 'at the back of the chapel' as the census enumerator termed it – next to the old Primitive Methodist Chapel. Flo, on her marriage to Lazzy, had left her employment at the Rectory and moved back in with her mother and with Ernest and her young son Fred. Flo and Ernest had three children, Nolan born in 1903, Gilbert born in 1906 and Elsie Elizabeth born in 1910. They all continued to live with Flo's mother

31

Elizabeth Heath and Flo's son Fred for some years, until the death of Flo's mother, and then Flo and Ernest Tubb and their family moved to Church Road, leaving Ernest's brother living in one of the thatched cottages on Hinton Road.

John Edward Church, owner of Home Farm and its 129 acres and tied cottages, was born in Southmoor but inherited land in Longworth from his father Richard, whilst his elder brother, also called Richard, lived at Heath House in Draycott Moor. John Edward lived at Home Farm with his elder sister Amelia and two servants. He never married and was considered by many locals to be rather a terrifying figure with a frightening presence – but Flo Heath always got on well with him – tongues wagged! He was known to subscribe to many of Longworth's charitable initiatives and was a member of the first Parish Council in Longworth.

John Edward Church
1849-1938

John Edward Church had taken his place in the community but of course mixed in very different circles from his tenants. In about 1915 after Amelia's death and when he was in his sixties he moved to Abingdon and let his house, and the farm, to Billy Bright who became the proxy landlord of the tenants of the Hinton Road cottages.

A painting of Home Farm circa 1881 at the time when John Edward Church was in residence. The photo below was taken in November 2012. The front cover shows a more distant view looking north from Hinton Road.

Flo Heath's sister Eliza Jane Richings was kept busy at home with a new baby arriving on average every eighteen months or so to add to her family. As a trusted village lady and mother of several children she knew what worked for the safety and well-being of mothers and babies, and in the absence of specialised training for General Practitioners at that time she became the official village midwife - for which she might have been paid at least in the form of expenses for transport.

She would have heard all the local gossip (including the talk about her sister, Flo Tubb, who had given birth out of wedlock) and she became well-known not only as the midwife but also as the layer-out of Longworth's dead.

Longworth High Street just before the Great War.
Right: Berkshire Supplies Store (Rant & Burgis).
Mid-distance left: The sign for the Crown Inn.
In the Square in the far distance: Webb's Store.

3. Wartime Sorrow

Bells, breakfasts and grumblers

In August 1914 at the onset of war the Bishop of Oxford asked that church bells should ring a muffled peal and Longworth and North Leigh bell-ringers both joined in the sad task with many others across the land. Nora Illingworth, the Rector's wife, wrote in Longworth Parish Magazine in August 1914:

"We are sure that everyone's heart and mind will be, as ours are, full of the War which is raging in Europe. We should like to have the names of all those who have volunteered for, or been recalled to, active service from Longworth."

She kept the village supplied with full details of the serving men and the losses encountered – there were to be many. Sorrow at the departure of friends and family and the oppressive thoughts that others would have to follow them were made worse for many by the long-term poverty of the area. The privations of the Great War, which were yet to come, must be set in the context of the existing poverty in Longworth at the start of the war. But Nora Illingworth was already on the job! She had written in her parish magazine in March 1914.

"It was represented to us before Christmas that it was nearly impossible for a labourer with a large family, at the present rate of wages combined with the large increase in the price of food, to provide really adequate food for all the children, even if he were perfectly steady. Of course, if this is not the case, the children suffer more. As an experiment, therefore, free breakfasts for the children of such labourers as cared to send them have been provided at the Rectory, Lady Hyde most kindly paying for them.

They are to be continued till the end of March. By that time less fire and light will be needed, and the difficulty will be less. An average of 18 children have come each morning, and we hope the experiment has been of use."

Mrs Hyde also arranged with the village bakers that during the winter months every family, where there were three children or more in a household, would receive bread at the same price as it was before the war and the widows and people too old to work should receive one hundredweight of coal each month. This and her weekly gifts of rabbits served greatly to lessen the distress in the area. Clothes for the poorest families in Longworth were regularly provided by the Berks and Bucks Needlework Guild. It contributed garments to a central depot in Windsor which then redistributed them to the member villages. Nora Illingworth was very firm about this:

"We would ask those of our friends who this year did not receive any of the clothing to remember that nearly all the things sent are for children . . . . grumblers are not a very amiable or attractive class of people, and we would fain hope there are few of them in Longworth."

Eliza Jane and her daughters took a turn at altering clothes which were too big or too small for those receiving them. And they, along with other ladies of the village, provided cakes regularly for wounded soldiers in Red Cross Hospitals in the region.

Harry and Flo
Harry and Flo Mansell, after their marriage, settled down to married life in North Leigh in November 1914. The early months of the Great War had brought neither a postponement of their wedding nor a delay in the start of their family.

But war would cast a heavy shadow over their initial happiness. Harry continued his employment with Bartlett Brothers in Witney but it was soon obvious that the Great War, far from being 'all over by Christmas', would need more men to fight in France and elsewhere. Harry and Flo faced an uncertain future and with their first child due in late November 1915 it would soon be time to make new plans. It was becoming clear that sooner or later Harry, now in his mid-twenties and older than the first soldiers to go to war, would have to enlist and leave home.

Harry and Flo closely followed news of the effects of the war on family and friends in Longworth. Postcards winged their way backwards and forwards and motorcycle-mad Harry journeyed between North Leigh and Longworth, alone when 'courting' and now with Flo after their marriage. There would have been no other way of managing the journey on a regular basis. Flo and Harry would also spend many of their weekends in residence in Longworth and knew everything that was happening. By mid-summer 1915, Flo, with her pregnancy advancing, was encouraged by her mother Eliza Jane, Longworth's midwife, to visit Longworth very regularly. Eliza Jane wanted her eldest daughter and first unborn grandchild in safe hands.

Harry Mansell and his motorcycle (circa 1915) which he used to commute between North Leigh, Witney and Longworth.

Flo planned to move back to her childhood home just for the birth of her baby under the shadow of certainty that both her brother Will and her husband Harry would go to war very soon. But Flo and Harry developed contingency plans in case Harry had to leave. On 1st December 1915, in Longworth, Flo gave birth safely to a son, Reginald William Leonard, who was baptised in Longworth church two days before Christmas. Longworth, with her midwife mother and two remaining younger sisters all there to support her, was an overwhelming attraction.

Gloom descends

Life in Longworth lost its vibrancy as many events were cancelled for the duration of the war. Nora Illingworth wrote in November 1914, 'We have not felt it right or seemly to arrange for ordinary entertainments and dances while this terrible war is on us. But Lady Hyde is most kindly arranging for a Lantern Lecture in the Rectory Barn and for some practices of patriotic songs, and ambulance classes are being given in the Rectory Barn.' Mrs Illingworth also organised help in Longworth for Belgian refugees - the village undertook to look after a family for three months in the first instance. Some of the assistance offered was in the form of vegetables, fruit and flowers rather than money. However, in all, the sum of £42 was raised by the village by the time the Fund was closed in 1915. Mercifully, the Belgian family they helped stayed in Oxford rather than suffer an Old Berkshire winter!

The Rector of Longworth, John Richardson Illingworth, by 1914-15 was much afflicted and worn down by a long term condition, psoriasis and its terrible effects. He often cycled backwards and forwards from Oxford where he gave regular lectures. He wrote to his friends about the effect the war was having in Longworth. 'We are strangely out of it all here, except for certain very vivid points of contact – the widows and wives in anxiety and one or two wounded home – and now and again a weekender from the Front at our eight o'clock service.'

Change was in the air and John Edward Church retired and left the village in 1915. He handed his farm over to a tenant, William (Billy) Bright who managed the land, which was for the most part rather difficult infertile sandy soil and he ran it at a low subsistence level – his crop production was very low indeed.

1915 was a bad year for Longworth – more and more young men went off to war and fewer and fewer came back on leave and even if they did come back it was years later and many returned maimed in mind or body. Rector John Illingworth was sent off to Kenilworth away from the pressures of the parish in the hope that his health would improve, but he died in August 1915 and his wife then had to give up her home and good works in Longworth. Nora Illingworth would be sadly missed - not least because the

detailed information in the Parish Magazines about the progress of local men at war soon drew to a halt.

Another indomitable lady, Mrs Crum from Longworth Manor Farm, who had done so much for the village, died. Mrs Crum and Nora Illingworth would be a very hard act to follow but Miss Edith Crum carried on her mother's good works and supported her father until his death in 1926. Nora Illingworth died in 1936.

Pressure mounts

The war was not going well for the allies and it soon became apparent that the first tranche of less than a million regular serving men and volunteers sent to the theatre of war would have to be massively supplemented. A large number of those already serving would be needed to train the raw recruits. Something had to be done. Conscription was not employed initially. Pressure to enlist for young men like Harry came from many quarters: employers, the threat of unemployment, posters in local streets, families and, not least, memories of seeing soldiers in training passing through villages like Longworth and towns like Witney long before the war. Large military exercises like the one in 1909 around Longworth increased the numbers of volunteers who enlisted in the new recruiting offices.

Army manoeuvres in Longworth (circa 1909), outside the Blue Boar in Tuck's Lane.

40

In September 1909 Rector John Illingworth wrote of the preparations for war:

"We are in great excitement. A big (mock) battle is going on around us, and all the neighbourhood is alive with troops, baggage waggons and field telegraphs. Yesterday a large party marched through Longworth and held it for a time, while they were searching for the enemy."

Sadly, thousands of men who presented themselves at recruitment offices, including some in Longworth and North Leigh, were not medically fit enough to fight. Childhood illnesses, poor education, poor diet and indifferent medicine racked up against them. This was a great indictment of an Imperial nation! More men (and women) needed to be targeted and the main message seemed to be that German atrocities could no longer be tolerated.

Conscription began in the spring of 1916. But by then Harry Mansell and Will Richings would have gone to war and Flo's cousin Fred Heath would be gone for good.

*The postcard caption reads:
Russian church bombarded by Germans.*

41

Front and reverse of a postcard sent 8pm 27 July 1915 from Masham Camp, Yorkshire (typed below for clarity).

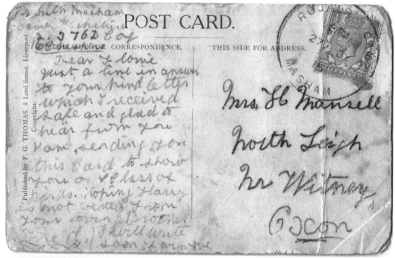

"Dear Florrie Just a line in answer to your kind letter which I received safe and glad to hear from you I am sending you this card to show you (our) class of Birds. Hoping Harry is not (vexed) From your loving Brother Fred. I will write soon if we move"

Crucially not enough thought, with enlistment strategies at full tilt, was given to the need for the maintenance of food production and other essential supplies and services and these were subject later to severe shortages even in villages like Longworth where the growing of food crops was well established. But crop yields were not nearly as high as they are today and without enough farm labour many crops went unplanted or unpicked. Prices rocketed. Those unwilling to enlist could use this as a basis for appeal. There were one or two conscientious objectors in Longworth but most available men prepared for war if they had not already done so. Harry Mansell and Will Richings signed on for the Army Reserve in December 1915 and a few weeks later they were both gone.

Flo Mansell's War

On Flo Tubbs' marriage to Ernest Tubb she had moved in with her mother, Elizabeth Heath. Her cottage, the other half of a semi, was next door to Jesse and Eliza Richings on Hinton Road. When Flo Tubb and her new family had grown too large for the cottage, they moved to another of John Edward Church's tied properties in Church Road. With the war on and no other workers available to rent the property, Flo Mansell, who had stayed mainly in North Leigh before the birth of her son, could now move into the vacated cottage. It would have felt good to be back in Longworth near her own family and in her own home at last, next door to her mother and sisters.

This small house was just right for Flo and baby Reg and, mindful of his safety and early infancy, she intended to remain there for the duration of the war - hopefully one that would be short and soon over. But Flo Mansell would have to settle down to years of life as a new mother without her husband at her side, like so many others in wartime. Leaving Longworth again would have been an impossibly huge wrench some years later when the war ended. Flo would never again live outside Longworth. It was directly as a result of the Great War that each of her children would live and die in Longworth and not in North Leigh.

It must have been hard to bear all the bad news of the war as it progressed. Harry and Will were away and they were full of anguish at the news that Flo's cousin Fred Heath had died in action. They grieved for the loss of such a young life. But Flo had a young baby to keep safe from successive measles outbreaks and other diseases stalking the very young. There was less and less to take Flo's mind off the worry - the sparkle went out of life in Longworth. The various seasonal entertainments along with children's church services, Sunday School and other gatherings in Longworth and elsewhere were regularly cancelled to prevent epidemics from spreading.

The parish magazine of January 1916 summed up the thoughts of many:

"The shadow of the Great War has cast a gloom over all our celebrations during this festive season, but it is hoped that in the hour of sorrow this glad festival has been the means of easing many an aching heart and brightening the sad homes that have been desolated by war."

Although Flo and her family observed the usual attendance at church for marriages and baptisms, it is not known if they were regular church-goers. Certainly many young married couples attended church more regularly and even joined confirmation classes during the war. Some families attended both church and chapel. Flo and her sisters certainly joined in the activities laid on at the Rectory and it is likely that they would have read the monthly parish magazines.

A new member of the family: Reg Mansell;
born December 1915.

Reg with his mother - his father was away at war.

Christening, January 1916
Standing: XX   XX XX XX Eliza Jane Richings XX
Front row: XX Flo Richings with Reg, Hilda Richings.

Flo played, as a young girl, with the sisters of many of the men going off to war, sharing interests in lace-making, hand-bell ringing, cooking and other pursuits with them too. These large families were close. Her mother, Eliza Jane, would have missed nothing in her daily cycle tours and routines.

There was a very strong community spirit in the village and with so many, like the Richings and other Longworth families, interrelated they all knew each other well. In the Great War this would have been greatly accentuated. Families were accustomed to loss of family and friends but mainly in the context of disease and old age and acceptance of the relatively short life spans of the time.

War was a nightmare, an obscene alien entity which took close friends, brothers, cousins and nephews even before they were out of their teen years. Fred Heath was only 18 when he was mown down in the trenches in 1915.

A postcard from Auntie Hilda to Master Reggie Mansell for his 2nd birthday in 1917 whilst his father was still away (note the gun).

All Birthday Joys

Good cheer be yours this happy day,
Good friends, good luck attend y
This simple, homely, kindly wish,
With all my heart, I s

Harry's War

With his wife often in Longworth during her pregnancy in the summer and autumn of 1915 Harry still had to go to work for Bartlett Bros in and around Witney so they could not easily move back to Longworth permanently – their intention was to be there only for the birth of their first child. In their first year of married life Harry's home village mirrored Longworth as younger friends and colleagues were leaving for training and then going abroad to face the enemy, but it was still the younger men who were enlisting in these early stages.

Some returned wounded or ill and others, lost or buried near the battlefields, did not return at all. More men would be needed for the hungry war machine. News from the Front got worse and then deteriorated yet again. The construction industry all but came to a halt with shortages and so many young men leaving for the Front and no one was planning in those uncertain times to have anything more than the most basic of repairs done to homes and businesses. There was a very real prospect of unemployment for many at this time. The need to join those going to war was becoming irresistible to those young enough to fight - and Harry had a war to fight.

His baby son having safely arrived at the beginning of December 1915, Harry responded to the notice he received to sign on for short service - for the duration of the war - and he was ready to go. Harry Mansell, aged 26 and ten months, was by all accounts one of the most unlikely men to fire a gun in anger. He was a gentle, pale, mild-tempered man of slight build, of shorter than average height at just over five feet five inches tall, with significant stomach troubles, of whom many said 'looked as though a puff of wind might knock him over'.

Harry Mansell's Enlistment Form; 11 December 1915. Harry was 26 years 10 months so on this form the army got his age wrong by 8 months.

In many recruiting halls family members, good friends and colleagues signed on together. This may have seemed like an adventure to some but to others it gave a strange confidence at a time of doubt. Harry went to enlist with Flo's brother Will Richings, seven years his junior, at their local recruitment centre in Witney on 11th December 1915. Will was a mason's labourer, still working for his father and he may well have worked with Harry. They certainly knew each other well by this time and they would each have given encouragement to the other when going to sign on. Some towns, particularly in the North and Midlands of England, unfortunately lost many of their men of military age at a single swoop when many men joined up at the same time as Pals battalions and fought and died together.

Harry Mansell (seated) and Will Richings (Flo's brother).

They enlisted together on the same day in December 1915.

Will stated that his employment was as a builder's mason, and Harry stated that his employment was 'slater and plasterer' with the firm of Bartlett Bros of Witney.

Harry Mansell first joined the Army Reserve for initial training and then was posted briefly to join the Somerset Light Infantry for further training on 10th April 1916 - but he was to serve in this Regiment for only 34 days. On May 13th he was attached to the Royal Warwickshire Regiment as a private and underwent further training at the Regiment's Depot in Birmingham until he left home soil for the first of four postings to the British Expeditionary Force in France where he saw active duty in the trenches around the Somme between 18th July 1916 and early August 1917. The postcard below seems to have neen sent on 9th October 1916.

The Cut-Out sections of this wartime postcard sent by Harry from 'somewhere in Europe' were removed by the censor. The card reads:

"My Dear Flo. Just a few lines to let you know I am quite well hoping this will find you all quite well from your ever loving Husband Harry X X X "

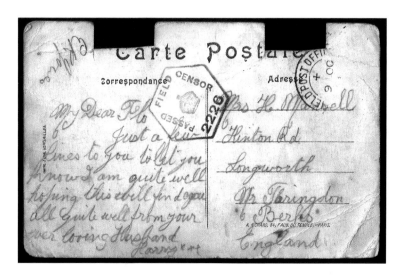

Other postcards followed in similar vein. However, some eight months later, on 8th August 1917, Harry suffered badly during a major gas attack and was treated initially at a local field hospital but after an assessment of the gas effects it was clear he could not continue his active service. He was sent back to his regiment's Depot near Birmingham to begin his recuperation.

Almost immediately Harry was sent from the Depot to a military hospital, an old barracks, at Buttevant on a 23-acre site halfway between Limerick and Cork in Ireland to recuperate. Here he was admitted to Ward Six which was full of men from his Regiment getting over the effects of gas inhalation – phosgene or mustard gas – and other conditions and injuries. The Germans (and the Allies) were using poisonous gases that killed thousands and resulted in chronic incapacity for so many others. The effects of the gas on Harry meant that he must have been feeling very ill as he travelled to reach Buttevant in the summer of 1917. He would have suffered acute fits of coughing, nausea, chronic fatigue, intense eye pain and damage to his mouth, lungs, stomach and intestines.

The caption on this card reads:
'Soldiers Home. Buttevant. Ireland'.

Harry and the other wounded men were assessed as to what further treatment they required and whether they could be discharged back to the Front or back home. But it was clear that Harry and many others wounded in the same gas attack had to remain for the foreseeable future.

A typical 'sleeping hut' in a 'convalescent camp'.

A group of patients with nurses at Buttevant.
Harry is in the back row on the right.

Harry had to have long-term treatment for inflammation of the stomach as well as for the other effects of gas inhalation. His chronic stomach problem, exacerbated by action in the trenches, was to trouble him for the rest of his life and indeed contributed to his relatively early death.

At Buttevant, in Ward Six, he spent a long time recuperating, as did so many others, by occupying himself with writing postcards home, a little light reading and with embroidery.

Harry found a very real interest in embroidery and produced several items, notably a belt commemorating the war (see overleaf). Some of Harry's work has been kept by the family for almost a century and this is now in the archives of the Longworth and District History Society.

Examples of embroidery by Harry Mansell during his convalescence. Left: a decorated belt. Above: the badge of the Royal Warwickshire Regiment.

A souvenir card listing the engagements of the Royal Warwickshire Regiment (6th Foot) in the Great War.

On the back of the card is written
"With love to my Dear Wife and Little Son.
From your loving Husband Harry XXXXX"

Keeping in touch

Long before the Great War those people separated from family and friends, even for a few days or hours, managed to keep in touch by mail - the most favoured and cheapest method being by postcard. Postcards were first 'invented' in 1869 in Austria and came across the continent to Britain the following year. They originally had no picture on the front as photo quality would have been very poor on such a small piece of low quality card. But experimentation took place and people's wish to send a quick note or to show how they had been able to take the sea air or take a break away from home soon pushed the numbers of these cards posted throughout Britain into the millions.

The Royal Mail had first allowed postcards to be sent in Britain in 1894 by which time a fast and highly efficient rail service was able to distribute postcards all over the country and indeed all over the world. Postcards became ubiquitous - cheap to buy and cheaper to send than ordinary letters (the card below cost just one halfpenny to post) and with several deliveries a day in most areas it became a national habit. By the time war broke out in 1914 it had become the norm to use postcards for every occasion. It was the heyday of the postcard, and they were not just sent on special occasions, informing friends and relations of a death in the family, or

in lieu of a Christmas or Birthday card, but also for the most mundane of reasons - to pass on a piece of even quite trivial chatter. Whilst it could never have been as convenient to send a postcard as picking up a phone or sending a text message, it could give a 'conversational' touch to communication. Interestingly in Harry's family it was usually the women who had most to say, but then for men writing whilst at war or in a convalescent hospital it was not easy to be verbose. Every small shop had a metal plaque declaring the sale of postcards. It was the mobile phone of the day! It could take just a few hours – less than a day - for a postcard to reach its destination – and so this was the best that could be done to send news, congratulations or condolences in haste in an age before telephones, fax machines or emails.

The two postcards, left, were amongst many received by Pte. H. Mansell during his long Buttevant convalescence. The card below shows German POWs captured early in the war, marching to Frith Hill Compound from Frimley Station near Aldershot. The card was sent from Aldershot to Longworth on 10 May 1915 by Harry Mansell, who enlisted in Witney seven months later on 11 December 1915.

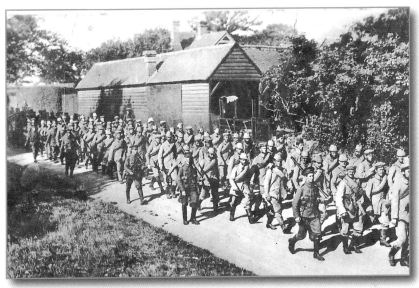

In wartime for those left behind, like Flo Mansell and her family, worrying and wondering what was going on, keeping in touch with loved ones was of the utmost importance. Telegrams were expensive and generally reserved for official purposes and would normally be dreaded during wartime. Servicemen and women at the Front were encouraged to keep in touch with home, and a thriving industry in postcards sprang up in towns and villages near the Front. Harry sent many cards home – often depicting local places showing the effects of the war. The Censor, of course, saw every card sent and would cut or blot out any fragments of information which could, if intercepted, give any clues as to the progress of the war or information about people and places.

For people like Harry and Flo who sent and received these cards it must have represented a very real lifeline. To receive a card from a relative at the Front meant that the sender was still alive – even if the still small voice within suggested that the passage of time might already be about to turn their lives upside down. For the sender writing a few words, on an easily available card provided for them, meant a moment or two to think of home and loved ones. The delight of postcards, particularly for those with short messages to send or for whom writing was not a welcome occupation, was that brevity was essential as the address took half the available space.

Education in most schools, certainly for ordinary people, was very basic and Harry Mansell, an artisan who left school at twelve or thirteen, certainly said very little in his postcards from the front – usually three sentences or rather short repetitive phrases at most. Some cards he sent relied entirely on the card alone to convey the message without the addition of a hand-written note! In any case the Censor would have kept a watchful eye on all his messages so it was never worthwhile to try say too much. Harry had to write in pencil - without the 'biro' or similar automatic ink pen which came later - it was the only writing equipment available for most people during the Great War. Harry's handwriting was clear and legible - despite being written either at the Front or convalescing in Ireland - the hand of a craftsman perhaps.

For special occasions like birthdays or Christmas Harry sent home from the Front a slightly more expensive silk embroidered card – but it was still very cheap. These cards were initially generated in Belgium where skill in stitched textiles was well-known but it spread across into France too – they were mass-produced by men and women on small sewing machines in homes throughout the region. The embroidered card (see five examples below) would normally have an envelope and a small printed card, sometimes carrying a handwritten message, could be tucked into the embroidered sleeve within. Most were simple messages or greetings but propaganda was also integral to many. These wartime postcards have become 'desirable collectors' items' – only stamps and coins are more collectible!

Back home and medals for Harry

Harry made a slow recovery from the worst effects of the mustard gas and it was to take over a year in hospital. It would have been virtually impossible to receive a visit from his family at home during that time, given travel restrictions, so postcards were essential. On 31st August 1918, just over a year after the gas attack which put him in hospital, he was keen enough and just about well enough to be discharged from Buttevant Military Hospital. He was given orders to proceed to his home, which from now on was to be Longworth, and there await further instructions.

Harry's discharge details quote that he had 'pulmonary fibrosis (tubercular) due to service'. His lungs and stomach were badly damaged after gas was used in the trenches. A history of years spent working with plaster and cutting stone tiles and smoking heavily (all his adult life) all exacerbated the problem caused by the scarring of his lungs in the trenches. After appearing in front of an Army Medical Board in Oxfordshire on 4th September 1918 he received his final official discharge - no longer physically fit for war service.

So even without the Armistice a few weeks later he would not have had to return to active service. He had served a total of 119 days in the Army Reserve and the Somerset Light Infantry and two years and 149 days with the Colours of the Royal Warwickshire Regiment – less than three years in the King's Army including his year in Buttevant.

It must all have seemed like a lifetime for a man such as Harry. Buttevant Military Hospital declined after the war was over and was later demolished and the site now lies under an industrial estate.

Harry was said by his commanding officers to have had 'a good war'. Only one comment of a less than perfect nature surfaced. He was once 'late on parade' - witnessed by a sergeant - for which he received five days confined to barracks. Harry's Certificate of Discharge was annotated in red with: 'Entitled to wear one Gold Wound Strip'. He was also given a character certificate carrying the legend, 'Bears a very good record'.

After his final discharge, in early September 1918, Harry applied to his nearest Post Office for the address of the Secretary of the local War Pensions Committee whose job it was to make provision for the care of disabled men after they left the service 'including provision for their health, training and employment.' Quite what initial support he received is not known. He certainly had to be admitted to hospital several times over the next few years for recurring stomach problems but with a wife and child to support and more children to follow, and with only a small army pension he aimed to pick up his trade as soon as he could.

Harry was said never to have been a well man after the war - and no wonder. He would have needed to continue his convalescence at home for many months. He had won a 'very good service' record and the award of the War Badge of the Royal Warwickshire Regiment dated 30th August 1918 for 'Services Rendered in H.M.'s Military Forces'. Harry was also honoured for his service in the British Expeditionary Force in France from 18th July 1916 to 20th August 1918. Whether this was any great consolation to him for the loss of the first few years of his married life and early fatherhood, his experience of the hellish trenches around the Somme, the loss of his health and the long, long fight to recover in hospital in Ireland, we will never know. Harry may well have counted himself lucky to return home at all!

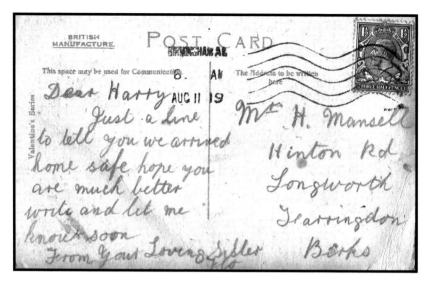

A postcard sent to Harry dated 11 August 1919 suggests that he was still not in very good health, two years after being gassed.

He became eligible for an army retirement pension when on his 'Notification of Final Award' for pension purposes his disability was noted as 'fifty per cent'. He was awarded a pension of 20 shillings (£1) plus 8/9d (about 44 pence) extra for his wife and (only) one child for life. Harry sought to enjoy a married home life, at last, with Flo and with Reg who were firmly established next door to Flo's parents, Jesse and Eliza Jane Richings. It must have been rather unsettling, on top of everything else to have gone to war, always having lived in North Leigh, and then many years later to go to Longworth to a new home, far from his original place of work and become father at last to a child who had grown from a tiny baby to a young lad now nearly three years old.

Impact of war on the family

Overall the Mansell and Richings families had pulled through the Great War in much better shape than many families had. Harry Mansell's brothers all survived the period of the Great War safely. Harry's brothers Albert and Fred had not had to enlist as they were considered too old to fight. His third brother Ivo enlisted in the Army Service Corps setting up supply lines for soldiers. Born in 1894 he was the youngest and he returned safely and lived until 1950.

Of Flo's family in Longworth, William Charles Richings (Will), the elder of Flo's two surviving brothers, had joined the Durham Light Infantry aged 19 years and seven months on the same day that Harry had joined up. They were sent off for training in different directions and having gone their separate ways they did not see each other again until after the war was over.

Will came back safely and took up his building and plastering career in partnership with his father and uncle, teaching his youngest sister's husband Fred Gutteridge, a general builder, the intricacies of plastering. Will left the village on his marriage to Ethel Weston. Flo's brother Sidney Ewart Richings had rather indifferent health which had kept him out of the war.

Sid did brick-laying and stonemasonry at first and he was a very handy man but was most interested in his milk round and later was able to buy a small plot of land in Butts Lane and rent further land to keep a few cows.

Fred Heath, Flo's cousin, a fine young man, a soldier in the 5th Battalion of the Royal Berkshire Regiment had died aged 18 in the trenches at Loos when his Battalion took many losses on 15th October 1915 - a sad end to a promising life.

His memorial stone at Loos says 'Remembered with honour'. His shocking early death rocked the village as well as the family. He was certainly very much missed in Longworth and Hinton. He had been a promising organist and was hard-working and highly capable. His mother, Flo Tubb, was of strong character but losing her eldest child at eighteen years of age must have hit her very hard. The news came just before the death of her mother Elizabeth Heath, who had cared for her grandson when Flo lived in at the Rectory and been so close to him – she was said to have been heart-broken. Flo's husband Ernest Tubb mercifully did not go to war. He was 34 when the war started and was a farm worker at Home Farm. He was known to enjoy a drink in his favourite pub, the New Inn, where his sister Flo Douglas worked.

Longworth's losses

Commemorative plaques and war memorials were erected and most of those who perished were listed on the village memorial where they had lived. But sometimes they appeared where their forbears lived or elsewhere. Family and friends, generations later, had to spend time searching for their loved ones' names in unexpected places.

The reasons for decisions as to where a serviceman or woman should be formally commemorated may be lost in the mists of time: some families may have worshipped in a church in a different village from where they lived, or the loved one may have lodged with different parts of the family or even with friends, some distance away.

Tragically, and perhaps inevitably with such large families (most had over six children), several families in Longworth including the Broughton, Hobbs, Leach, Newport, Rivers and Webb families - many of whom were close friends of the Mansell and Richings families - lost more than one son or close relative.

The impact of Longworth's losses on local businesses, such as Prince's Rose Grounds and some of the larger farms, was particularly devastating when skilled men were lost. Local resident Miles Drew was to say much later, 'In the first war it was very bad round here, lots of villagers lost three from their homes and any amount of twos. The first war hit the village hardest because in the second war the generals weren't allowed to have the men off the land that would produce food. We'd come very near to starvation.'

Hard times and dogged determination

Most of the work on offer in Longworth was still on the farms but coping with the privations of the painfully slow post-war recovery, the Great Slump of the 1920s as well as the Depression of the 1930s, was a nightmare for farmers and other employers. Farmers tried everything they could to earn their own living and also keep men employed.

Many men in Longworth had not returned and those who had were often sick, maimed or disorientated – for example Ray Dunsdon's father, James, living at Prince's Row on the Square, who was never able to work full time again after the war despite having six children to care for.

A large acreage of land in Longworth was planted with fruit trees, mostly apples and pears, and what had been Langham's Farm in Sudbury Lane became Sudbury Fruit Farm. Indeed the whole village seemed full of fruit trees! But later with the advent of imported apples these became unprofitable and the trees were grubbed up and as Nigel Drew remarked, 'the only scrumping available to village boys was in the small orchards of Tommy Dewe's at Coltons on Tuck's Lane and those of Henry Drew's Church Road property.'

There were other initiatives in the village too – all of mixed fortunes. A 26-acre pine wood planted by Sir Clarendon Hyde, an ex-MP and businessman of Longworth House along Lodge Lane, later led to the lane having its name changed, at least the lower part, to Pine Woods Road. Hyde intended the plantation to be a pension for his son but it was never to be - Anthony Hyde died tragically young in the Second World War and 28 years after the wood was planted Tony Slade felled it to plant annual crops.

4. Family Life in Longworth

Although they were by no means well off, Harry and Flo in the twenty-year period after the Great War, were for the most part very happy, despite all that had gone before. Together again with Flo and Reg, after the separations and exertions of the Great War, Harry attended hospital regularly and regained a reasonable degree of health and fitness but his health was certainly never again robust. Working in the context of the grim economic conditions of the time, he had to make the best of things. His small army pension would not have gone far with their growing family but he had a trade and that was important for the family's survival.

Harry, when well enough to work at least part-time, found employment locally in Longworth. In those days, in rural areas like north Berkshire, a seven-mile journey to work was too far to travel every day so Harry could not consider taking up work again with his former employers, Bartlett Bros of Witney. Flo was near her family for good. Jesse Richings was in his late fifties and his generation of builders and plasterers were reaching an age when they might have to take work more steadily and hand over to younger men - skilled men like Harry Mansell would always be needed.

Harry had excellent skills as a plasterer, a Stonesfield slater and as a general builder and he was available to work for anyone who would employ him in the Longworth area. He re-joined his Trade Union association – now rather grandly called the National Association of Plasterers, Granolithic and Cement Workers. But, despite the fact that so many homes were in dire need of repair and maintenance, the building trades, like many others after the war were somewhat dislocated. Workers, like Harry, often needed to build up their strength and fitness and money was scarce - relatively few people were in a position to have much work done on their properties and building materials were in short supply in part because of rundown transport systems. The slow pace of available jobs would, however, have suited Harry's requirement not to overdo it whilst he recovered from the long-term effects of his wartime experience.

Mansell Children

On 29th December 1919, when Reginald was four, a second son, Frederick George Mansell was born to Harry and Flo. Tragically a year later, in December 1920, Flo's father Jesse Richings fell off his bicycle on rough ground in Longworth and a few days later, without regaining consciousness, he died, aged 58. More happily in 1921 a daughter, Isobel Irene, known as Betty, was born to Harry and Flo. The photographs of this period give an impression of a very happy family life attended by a succession of much-loved dogs.

Flo, Betty, Harry and Fred, with motorcycle.
Note the carbide gas lamp that burnt acetylene
created by the reaction of calcium carbide with water.

Children grow up! A glimpse into the family album.

Betty   Fred   Reg

Longworth School 1930
Fred is on the far left of the central row.

The children grew up at the cottage on Hinton Road and played out in the roads or over the fields when not at the village school behind the Congregational Chapel in the centre of the village. It was an un-denominational school and had no religious affiliation – but there was Bible study and most of the Bibles and hymn books in the school actually came from the chapel. Virtually all the children in the village at this time, their fathers, mothers and even grandparents had attended the school and so would their own children and cousins and their children and grandchildren after them. All three Mansell children were lively and outgoing – probably much more so than either of their parents and they always seemed to draw in other children from the village to wherever they happened to be. Harry worked away at his plot of land behind Squirrel Cottage, rented from Home Farm, as soon as he was fit enough after the war. He kept the soil fertile by the regular deposits of 'night soil' from the trenches behind the cottages. He would always try to grow as much as his plot could support and stored the root vegetables in clamps to last the winter and spring until the next season's crop was ready.

Reg, Fred and Betty Mansell and many other village children had their school lunches, on days when they didn't run home for lunch, in the Village Institute. They may have been served food cooked by Winnie Drew and dished out by Dolly Hobbs - both ladies lived in Church Road, Longworth. The Village Institute (at first called the Men's Institute) played a vital part in village life - Iris Carter's mother (later to be a close neighbour of the Mansells) was the caretaker during the 1930s and 1940s. Flo Mansell's sister Hilda continued her Girl Guide meetings there too and most young people would have their wedding reception there. The dinners were served in the main hall where a stage had been constructed at the road end and there was a sectioned off area at the back which served as a billiard room. Films were projected through a hole in the partition. Harry Mansell took a role on the Village Institute committee.

Unfortunately, many years later in 1964, one of Harry's sons was cycling past the Institute when he noticed the hall was on fire – he pedalled away to get help but the village institute days were over. It was some years before another hall rose from the ashes.

With their Aunt Hilda very much involved with the Girl Guides it was not surprising that both Reg and Fred joined the Boy Scouts. There was a thriving troop in Longworth, which met in the barn next to the Manor. It was an early pioneer of scouting as former residents of Longworth Manor, the Crums, had been long-term friends of the Chief Scout Robert Baden-Powell. He, as a good friend of the Waltons too, continued to visit the Manor frequently usually staying in what became 'the camping field'. But after a while Reg found other more compelling interests, while Fred appears to have done rather more with the Scouts. With its emphasis on outdoor pursuits the Scouts would have been an ideal 'hobby', particularly in an interwar society where money was in short supply. Like generations of sons before, both boys were encouraged to share their father's involvement in the building trade.

The late Miles Drew considered Harry to have been a fine cricketer, despite giving every appearance of frailty and suffering with his chronic lung and stomach trouble. Nigel Drew who had had long conversations with his father Miles said,

"Harry was a stalwart of the local team with many wickets to his credit. My father played regularly in teams which included Harry and had a high regard for his prowess. The cricket was played all over North Berkshire and South Oxfordshire. Most of the teams would have worked until lunchtime on a Saturday and then cycled up to ten miles to an opponent's ground. It was amazing that any of these men (especially, perhaps, Harry) could stand up let alone play the sorts of innings and take the number of wickets which they actually managed. Then of course they all had to cycle home."

These men were all made of stern stuff!

Fred's personal Scout health card with a table on the back to enter regular height, weight and chest measurements which can then be compared with 'healthy boys'.

BOY SCOUTS

STANDARD MEASUREMENTS

AGE	HEIGHT	WEIGHT	CHEST (EMPT
10	4 ft. 3·84 in.	4 st. 11·5 lb.	26·10 in.
11	4 ft. 5·50 in.	5 st. 2 lb.	26·53 in.
12	4 ft. 6·99 in.	5 st. 6·7 lb.	27·20 in.
13	4 ft. 8·91 in.	5 st. 12·6 lb.	28·03 in.
14	4 ft. 11·33 in.	6 st. 8 lb.	28·46 in.
15	5 ft. 2·24 in.	7 st. 4·7 lb.	29·74 in.
16	5 ft. 4·31 in.	8 st. 7 lb.	31·53 in.
17	5 ft. 6·24 in.	9 st. 4·9 lb.	33·64 in.
18	5 ft. 6·96 in.	9 st. 11·4 lb.	34·19 in.

The above are the Standard Measurements of a healthy boy. If you are below the standard you should go in for a course of training. You would find some of the following Charts very useful. They can be obtained from Headquarters at 3d. each, postage any six, 1s. 10d. free.

1. How to be Healthy
2. Wrist and Arm Exercises
3. Leg and Trunk Exercises
4. Abdomen and Leg Exercises
5. Dumb-Bell Exercises
6. Indian Club Exercises
7. Ju Jitsu
8. Rescue from Fire
9. Rescue from Drowning
10. How to Act in Other Emergencies (including Horse Bolting, Escape of Gas, Ice Breaking)
11. How to Prevent Consumption
12. Quarter Staff Play
13. Knots, Hitches, and Bends
14. Morse Signalling Code
15. Semaphore Signalling Code
16. Simple Bandaging
17. Sick Nursing
18. Swimming
19. Figure Carving
20. Boxing
21. Stencils and Stencilling
22. Hammock Making, etc.
24. Scout Staff and its Use
25. Fretwork
26. Camp Cookery
27. Model Aeroplane
28. Badges of Rank in Navy
29. Badges of Rank in Army
30. Club Room Hints
31. Tent Making
32. Camping Hints

Also, Fires for Cooking—Seamanship Code Flags, &c.—The Compass —Life-Saving by Rocket Apparatus — Pioneering and Bridge Building — Field Sketching.

Growing the business

Harry worked on as a slater and plasterer but most of his work was as a general builder. He refurbished old stone properties and patched up any redbrick houses in the area. But there were still very few of those about at this time. He established a local clientele and a good reputation for doing an excellent job. He worked at the Blue Boar, the New Inn and the Lamb & Flag, as well as all the big houses in the area. In 1927, with his health improved and whilst the children were still quite young, Harry, though he used a handcart for local jobs, bought a small lorry and established his own business - 'H. Mansell' - a building firm which also did general haulage where required. Whichever vehicle was in use the family dog was usually in attendance. Harry and his lorry (and the dog) were responsible for the transport of a wide range of items - from building materials for himself and other builders to dead-stock such as pigs, or indeed anything heavy which needed collecting from local railway stations - mainly from Challow or Wantage Road stations - or from one of the nearest towns.

H. MANSELL: Building, Decorating, Stonesfield Slating, Plastering, Stonewalling,Crazy Paving, Rockeries, Garden Vases and General Repairs.

School-leavers

Fred, Mum (Flo) and Reg

The children all left school when they reached fourteen as was normal then and Reg stayed in Longworth picking up the threads of his father's business, gradually becoming more and more involved with plastering and eventually going on the payroll, but his first love was engineering and he would have loved to do that full time. But it was not to be.

Fred, when he was 16 at the end of 1935, started an apprenticeship as a carpenter for W.A. Wheeler & Co., a large firm of builders and contractors in Wantage. He would have cycled each way and as a teenager he thought nothing of nipping home after work for tea and then cycling back to Wantage to go to the cinema. Six-monthly reports were sent home by Wheelers along with requests for the next part of the apprenticeship premium of £5.00.

One report stated, 'Your son Frederick now seems to have settled down to his job and should make a very good carpenter.' Another report stated, 'The lad seems to be making good progress and likes his job.' Fred received weekly wages of 10/- (50 pence) in the first year, 14/- (70p) in his second year, 17/6 (about 87p) in his third year, 21/- (£1.5p) in his 4th year and 27/6 (about £1.37

pence) in the final year of his apprenticeship. For these wages Fred worked nine hours a day for the full term of five years and promised to conduct himself as 'an honest and faithful apprentice'.

On finishing his apprenticeship Fred joined his brother and came to work for his father, specialising in carpentry work. With Reg taking on the general building work and Harry focussing where he could on plastering and tiling they had a wide range of skills to offer. Harry never changed the name of his business from H. Mansell to H. Mansell & Sons but the business continued until Fred retired.

This postcard posted on 9 August 1921 with a penny ha'penny stamp, was sent to Master R Mansell with a simple message "best love from V. Ludow". For us the main interest is perhaps a deserted Longworth Square. A pony and trap stand outside the Blue Boar. The General Supply Stores and Post Office has large window adverts for chocolate and Cadbury's Cocoa.

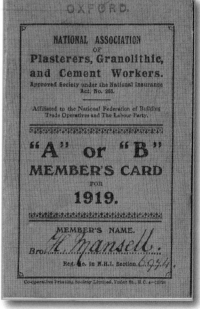

Above: Harry Mansell (seated on the far left) was a member of the Men's Institute, of Longworth, seen here gathered outside the Village Hall in the early 1930s.

Right: Harry was also a member of the National Association of Plasterers, Granolithic, and Cement Workers which he had joined in 1913.

The card notes that the 'Contribution per week to General & Superannuation Funds' was 9d.

The Richings family

Flo's mother Eliza Jane Richings lived on into her seventies in her old family home - the adjoining cottage next door to Flo and Harry. Her daughter Hilda stayed even after her marriage in 1928 because her husband was in the Royal Navy until 1931 and away a great deal. From then until the war he was in the Royal Navy Volunteer Reserve and as such was called up only for two weeks every two years for training. Hilda's brother Sid remained there until after his mother died. Eliza Jane was a much-loved grandmother, though she would never live to see all eleven of her children's children. She was, by all accounts, quite a character and rather indomitable (unlike her eldest daughter Flo who had a much more retiring nature) and she achieved notoriety as a woman with her own transport. As village midwife and layer-out of the dead she needed to be able to get to outlying cottages quickly if a mother was in the late stages of labour or if someone had just died.

Midwife Eliza Jane Richings on her rounds.

She at first travelled around by pony and trap and later by tricycle. She apparently disliked two-wheelers as she had a tendency to fall off! After her old pony died she had an Austin 7 – a popular little car which the youngsters of the family referred to jokingly as 'Gran's Tin Lizzie'. The Americans had produced a Model T Ford car, that had a huge market in the United States, which was frequently seen in the movies and referred to as 'Tin Lizzie'. The only family drivers initially were Eliza Jane's son Will who had moved away from the village and her daughter Hilda's husband Fred. But she set herself to the task and learnt to drive.

Eliza Jane's grandson, Stan Gutteridge, remembers:

"Occasionally, on summer evenings, the whole lot of us would be ferried to a pub such as the Noah's Ark at Frilford - three at a time. So many trips! As soon as we were all at the pub it was time to start returning the first of us back home again! We referred to this car as 'Gran's old Tin Lizzie' but it was only about seven years old. Some years later it was quite a shock to realize that my own first car was 22 years old!"

Flo's younger brother Sid kept a herd of cows with his Uncle Albert (Uncle Put) up the road. Albert Richings, who mixed his work as a general stonemason with producing and selling milk, had no sons to take on his stonemasonry or the business of delivering milk in and around Longworth. Sid took over the milking, from the 1920s. Milk was delivered twice daily direct to the door. Sales of milk far outside the village, before the milk collection service by tanker came in, would not be possible. The big churns of milk could not easily be carried even to the nearest railway station. Local lads of the day such as Ray Dunsdon still recall Sid Richings and 'Porky' Brooks, amongst others, 'riding round Longworth on their bikes with two large milk cans on the handlebars.' Sid had not gone off to the Great War as his health was not good and he remained at the cottage on Hinton Road and eventually not enjoying living alone after his mother died, in 1938, he married Cis (Teresa) Wiggins whose parents ran the Blue Boar in Tuck's Lane.

Flo's youngest sister Hilda Richings, living with her mother through most of the 1920s, had several jobs in the area. In 1919 when she was working in the Post Office in Faringdon she had an amazing job offered to her. A Longworth School manager, probably Mrs Hyde from Longworth House, came in to see her, 'We need a new junior school teacher and you are it.' An old pupil at the school, Hilda was enrolled as an assistant teacher for the next seven or eight years where she taught the infants and thoroughly enjoyed herself - she was clearly up to the job.

Hilda Richings (far left). Longworth Junior teacher.

But all married women teachers in those days had to give up work and so on marrying Fred Gutteridge from Canterbury in Kent she had to leave teaching. Hilda and Fred had met because Fred's Aunt was Ada Nichols' housekeeper at Haugh House in Church Road, Longworth and from the age of twelve Fred used to visit Longworth. They were married on 9th April 1928. Their wedding photograph includes Mrs Hyde the district Guide leader who was keen to involve Hilda in her Guiding work, and also shows the licensees of the Royal Oak as well as family members. Many absent members of the family had to work and could not be present.

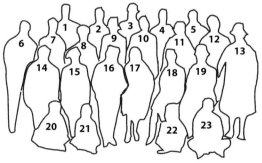

1928 wedding guests of Hilda and Fred Gutteridge.

Numbered guests listed overleaf.

81

1928 Wedding of Hilda and Fred Gutteridge. Photo-list.

1   Sid Riching's bride's brother
2   ? Green of Rose Cottage, Tuck's Lane
3   Agnes Richings - bride's sister
4   Gilbert Tubb (Flo's cousin)
5   Harry Mansell
6   George Harding - licensee of the Royal Oak
7   Hilda Harding - wife of George
8   Ethel Richings (née Weston)
9   Elsie Green (wife of number 2)
10 ? Frank Patrick - later = husband of Agnes Richings
11 Mrs Hyde of Longworth House
12 Will Richings - bride's brother
13 Flo Mansell
14 Albert Richings (Uncle Put) - bride's uncle
15 Amy Drayton - bridesmaid
16 Fred Gutteridge - bridegroom
17 Hilda Gutteridge (née Richings) - bride
18 Edi Drayton - bridesmaid
19 Eliza Jane Richings?
20 Cyril Peveril (Hilda Harding's son)
21 Fred Mansell
22 Betty Mansell
23 Reg Mansell

Hilda and Fred's first son Stanley Ewart Gutteridge (Stan) was born at Wickham Cottages in November 1929. He was the last but one of the Richings family children to be born on Hinton Road and he would be six months old before his sailor father saw him. Fred's own father before him had been a serviceman so Fred thought nothing of going away. Family memories indicate that Fred's father had fought in the Indian Army and spent seven years on board ship.

He lost his first wife who left five boys to be looked after. Later he fell through a skylight and was accused of trying to commit suicide, but in truth he had already found another woman to marry and share the work of bringing up the boys!

Hilda moved out of her family home on Hinton Road in 1931 when Fred stood down from the Navy and they moved with their toddler son, Stan, to Little London on Faringdon Road in Southmoor. Hilda settled into her new family home which was a very small cottage at Little London - one of a row of five converted from a former mill on marshy land to the west of the village of Southmoor (then called Draycott Moor). Fred picked up work as a general builder with Harry and then his brother-in-law Will Richings taught him plastering at Longworth Manor.

Leaving Hinton Road

A harbinger of change came in 1937 when Flo Mansell's mother Eliza Jane Richings that well-known figure, always out and about on her 'vehicle of the moment' tending expectant mothers and laying out the dead, died aged 71. This heralded a period of great change for the Mansell and Richings families and indeed the village.

John Edward Church died aged 88 in Abingdon in early 1938. The Home Farm Estate was then prepared for auction with vacant possession. Everyone at Wickham Cottages was given notice to quit as they had no entitlement to their tied cottage. Billy Bright, the farmer who rented all of John Edward Church's Home Farm house and its entire estate, went to live in Charney Bassett and so Home Farm, its 129 acres and two pairs of tied cottages in Hinton Road were put up for sale with vacant possession on 12th September 1938 at the Queen's Hotel in the market square at Abingdon.

Other properties in Church Road were withdrawn from sale just before the auction most probably because the tenants bought their freehold. Ernest Tubb's brother, at Squirrel Cottage worked on the farm so he remained, as did his neighbour Mr Stratford who was a carter. Sid Richings and his new wife Cis and baby son Peter moved initially into the Blue Boar where Cis's parents lived. Then they went to live at Little London with Sid's sister Hilda and her family.

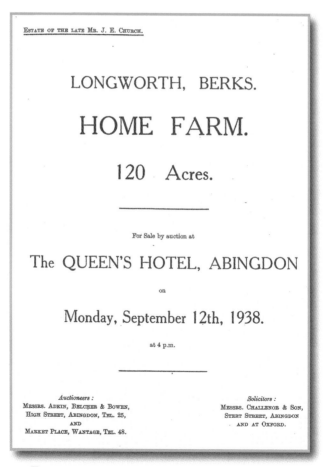

Home Farm auction. See map, inside rear cover.

The legacy of Home Farm auction

There was plenty of spare housing capacity in the area. Coincidentally, Donald Prince, landowner and proprietor of George Prince's Oxford Roses in Tuck's Lane, Longworth, was preparing to leave the area at about the same time Edward Strauss at Kingston House in Kingston Bagpuize went bankrupt in 1936. Almost every cottage in Tuck's Lane and some in Church Road and The Square in Longworth, as well as many others in Kingston Bagpuize, came on the market.

Despite the fact that many of the houses had sitting tenants who were not required to move, there was a great deal of change for the families in the two neighbouring villages in the late 1930s. Fred Broughton bought up many acres of the Prince's land and property in Tuck's Lane but most of the rest of the leasehold homes, once under the ownership of Church and Strauss, went to new families.

The Home Farm estate was bought almost in its entirety by Tony Slade who had moved from his family's farm in Compton, south of Didcot, in 1937 where a slump in corn prices had hit the family fortunes. He bought a bungalow at Spring Hill just off the Faringdon Road further south in the parish of Longworth. At the 1938 auction he bought everything that had originally been Home Farm lands and properties, with the great exception of the big house with its outbuildings and paddock which went to a Mr Gearing.

Tony Slade in his field on Frilford Farm, behind Wickham Cottage.

Tony described the 129 acres of land he bought as 'derelict'. Indeed Stan Gutteridge's description was similar:

"Farming was in the doldrums and poor old Billy Bright used to plough a bit here and there. When I was a kid most of the land south from Hinton Road down to the withy beds and to the Faringdon Road was just heathland. It was unfenced; it was rough, unkempt land and Billy used to just turn out a few sheep and cattle here and there. On a bit of the land he planted a few potatoes here and corn there, but it was mostly subsistence farming - growing their own food and just enough of a crop to pay the rent. That was the only outgoing they had to pay."

Tony Slade bought the farmland for £12 per acre and then installed drainage and irrigation systems, having persuaded his bank to back him as he had no money of his own at that stage. He added to the quota of tied houses and farm buildings by building new properties. Tony also bought land where Millets Farm Centre now stands in Frilford but he later sold this at a time when the future for pig farming and horticulture in the area looked bleak. His holdings went under the name of Frilford Farms.

Church Road

In summer 1938 Harry and Flo Mansell after 24 years of married life moved with their three children from Hinton Road, where Flo and at least two previous generations of her family had been born. They moved with their children Reg, Fred and Betty who by this time were aged 22, 18 and 16, respectively, to a thatched, terraced cottage in Church Road, Longworth. The row of four thatched stone cottages stood next to the allotments on the north-east side of the road. The thatch, like most of its kind before wire mesh was routinely laid on top of it, was home to dozens of sparrows, swifts and martins. The whole block of cottages later became known as 'Longworth House' from the early 30s- the name once given to the large house along Lodge Lane where the Hyde family lived.

The two terraced cottages at the allotment end had front doors facing the street and the other two had front doors at the back! During the late thirties, when Harry and Flo moved in, the cottages nearest the allotments housed Charles and Beatrice Carter and their two daughters Iris and Sadie. They lived next door to the Jones family, then next door again lived Harry and Flo and their three children and then a Miss Painton. Iris Graham, née Carter, who lived close to Harry and Flo from her birth in 1938 through much of her childhood, remembers the Mansells.

'They were lovely. I was always toddling in. Flo was a very quiet lady – a real countrywoman. I got to know their son Reg best as he was home more. Betty Mansell was working each day and Fred was working outside the village and later went away.'

Harry and Flo's new cottage - part of 'Longworth House' in Church Road

There was a long garden for each cottage with a privy at the end, tucked behind a laurel hedge. Children of the cottage families, like Iris, would have the job on wet days of cutting up newspaper for use in the privies, and the eldest son (like Reg Mansell) usually had to help the father empty the 'night soil' and spread it into a trench in the allotments – a job usually done at dusk or in the dark. The allotments with such ready supplies of 'compost' must have been highly productive. Iris Graham remembers that the crops were very much the same as today with lots of potatoes and other root crops, with potatoes stored in clamps from the previous year. There were plenty of peas and runner beans but nothing as fancy as French beans or sweet corn. Flowers, fruit, salad crops and herbs such as mint were grown in the cottage gardens.

Young boys of the family, like Hilda's son Stan Gutteridge, loved to 'help Uncle Harry'. For some reason Harry delighted in growing 'tons' of onions which required a great deal of hand-weeding. Stan remarked:

> *"There was one bloody weed which grows between onions - stinging nettles! The very idea of wearing gloves in a garden then would have branded you a cissy for a lifetime."*

Harry bought the fruit of several orchards and his nephews willingly helped pick the fruit. There were cottage garden shows held most years in Longworth or another nearby village and most families would have joined in and shown off their vegetables and fruit. The vegetable tops and peelings, plus any food slops from the house were recycled. (There was no dustbin collection or recycling lorry in those days.) In Harry and Flo's garden there was the family pig – the ultimate recycler. Harry organised a Pig Club and friends contributed towards the cost of the pig, feeding it and then slaughtering and were rewarded with a share of the meat. When the time came to kill the pig, usually in the autumn, the village pig killer, Bart Painton's son of Butts Lane, went round the village dispatching the pigs, cutting up the carcasses, and salting them ready for the families to swap pieces among themselves and their friends and neighbours. Some of the meat was eaten fresh but most was smoked or salted for future use. The pig blood was collected in a bucket ready for making black puddings. Mrs Painton sold many of these from her home at Well Cottage in Butts Lane. Her ceiling was hung with many a dozen 'rounds' of puddings. Bacon sides, further payment for her husband's work as local pig-killer, also hung around the smoky fireplace.

Fun and work in the fields

These years just before the Second World War certainly seemed rather idyllic as far as Flo and Harry's children and nephews were concerned. Reg tinkered away for years with model traction engines and later set up a steam engine in a workshop in Butts Lane. Thus engines

of one kind or another became a major interest and as each boy grew older, motorbikes became of greatest interest. The only four-wheeled vehicle they ever owned was the builder's lorry but later they lovingly tended their motorbikes and both bought machines which thrilled the young lads of the village.

Harry (left) with Betty and Reg, now young adults.

Fred, Betty and Reg Mansell.
"Motorbikes become of great interest." Their's was
an 'Excelsior', a popular bike in the mid-30s.

Customers in the village in later years noted, often with some resignation, that the Mansells always stopped work on the dot of 4 o'clock, probably perfectly fair given that builders always start in early morning. This was 'their' time when they rode the bikes up and down the road and tinkered with them whilst Harry joined in or spent time on the allotment.

Tony Gutteridge, remembers hay-making on his Uncle Sid Richings' fields:

"The whole family turned out - Uncle Harry, Auntie Flo, Auntie Aggie and Uncle Frank (Flo's sister and brother-in-law who had moved to Oxford from Coventry) and everybody helped - all the women with long wooden rakes, raking the hay, the men forking the hay onto the wagons borrowed from Fred Broughton. About five o'clock Auntie Flo came up with the tea and we sat down in the field. In the early days, before she died Gran (Eliza Jane Richings) would come too. It was cold tea because you didn't dare light the fire in the field in the middle of summer."

These fields, where Sid kept his cows, lay beside Longworth House down Lodge Lane and were rented from the Hyde family. Sid also rented land on the Home Farm paddock. He was able to buy a small strip of land along Butts Lane after the Home Farm auction and here he kept a cow or two and some chickens (see map inside back cover). At the end of the holding was the postman's hut where the postman could have an hour or two's rest before starting back to Faringdon with the evening mail at 5.35pm six days a week.

5. All at War Again

The blight on plans

The latter part of the 1930s, from outward appearances, certainly seemed a good time to be in Longworth, cut off as it was from most of what was happening in Europe and the build-up to the Second World War - not every household had a radio, even then! But as the 1930s drew to a close, it looked as though Harry in his late-fifties (an age he might not have envisaged reaching back in 1917) and Betty, now in her late teens, would have to do war work of some kind. Reg and Fred would have to be ready to be called up for active service at any moment. Flo Mansell's health was not good and Harry was still not considered to be a fully well man. Perhaps his gaunt appearance and quiet approach to life enhanced this view. Harry carried on his building work with the help of his sons, continued to support village concerns and grew vegetables for the family and looked after the livestock in the garden.

The Ministry of Food, mindful of the grave food shortages during and after the First World War, was placing all sorts of restrictions on marketing and movement of food of all kinds. Britain had to become much more self-sufficient in every commodity. The men became worried that major restrictions would be placed on haulage and building trades too.

Builders require a dedicated builder's yard or at least a dumping ground for the general bric-a-brac kept for future use, a space for a vehicle and lock-up space - but space was at a premium at Church Road. The cottage had no front yard and the backyard was full of produce – salad vegetables, soft fruit, a pigsty and a well, and access was through a neighbour's garden.

So the family looked around for a builder's yard. Harry had long wanted a bigger house for the family and he was very much aware of the derelict property, No 2, Butts Lane. He asked the Waltons of Longworth Manor whether they would rent out the property. The house was in a parlous state with bushes growing out of the walls. The owners were willing to rent but Harry eventually wanted to purchase the property, with the prospect of another war looming however, he could do little for the present. He was able to use the ground around the house as a builders' yard and a place to park the lorry and turn the lean-to shed at the side into a workshop. Restrictions had been put on the availability of materials and the amount of money which could be spent on constructing or refurbishing a house.

It would be 1947 before he would obtain the freehold of the property and start making the house habitable - but they had by then improved the old lean-to which they later rebuilt as a garage and Reg could tinker with his steam engine. There was some talk that the house was used as a shooting butts during wartime in the past – harking back to a time when every settlement had archery butts, which is probably how Butts Lane came by its name.

Dark shadows of another war

It would be a worrying time yet again for Harry and Flo and all their wider family in the village; they lived under great apprehension wondering who would be the first in the family to go to war. In fact the first to be called up, in 1939, was Navy Reservist Fred Gutteridge, Flo's youngest sister's husband. One morning, ready to leave to go aboard ship, he called at Longworth School to say goodbye to his children. They didn't see him again until 1945!

Stan's brother Tony remembered:

"My first memory of the Second World War is hearing a knock on the school door about 10 o'clock one morning and then a familiar voice saying, 'Sorry to bother you, Miss Simpson, but could I please say goodbye to my children.' My father had received his calling up papers through his place of employment. He was posted to Archangel, in Russia, for a long while on convoy reception duties. When Dad was away during the war Uncle Harry (Mansell) was our father-substitute."

Uncle Ernest Tubb (top left) standing next to Fred Gutteridge with Fred's three children, Stan, Tony and Marina.

During the early part of the war it must have been a tight fit in Hilda's two-up two-down cottage at Little London, despite Fred's absence. Not only were there her three children but also Sid, Cis and their son Peter, all crammed in. Everyone was poor - there were more orange boxes than actual pieces of furniture. However, family was family and there was no shortage of good times. Both Hilda and later her daughter Marina played the piano and everyone had a sing-song most nights during the war.

Sid and Cis were able to move out when their search for a home of their own ended in 1942 when they moved to the east cottage at Barn Ground opposite Laburnum Cottage, leaving Hilda alone with her three children until after the end of the war in 1945.

Fred served part of his time on HMS Walpole. This was an Admiralty V Class Destroyer first launched in 1918. In Fred's time it was in the Second Destroyer Flotilla – part of the Atlantic Fleet on convoy defence duty. The ship was lost after it flooded badly following a hit from an exploding floating mine. It was taken by tug to Chatham Docks and declared a total loss and broken up in 1945.

Keeping food on the table

It was the women, like Flo and Betty Mansell, who bore the brunt of the struggle to put enough food on the table when shortages and rationing started. Half the food bought at the shops was imported and sea convoys, bringing a range of essential food and other goods, became major targets so rationing was essential. The weekly order from Free's shop in Longworth was awaited with trepidation and they would wait to see what meat and 'extras' they could have. Betty would spend time queuing on occasion but the grapevine in Longworth served the local women well and new deliveries were pounced on very quickly. Hilda's children, Tony and Stan, waited even more eagerly to see what the sweet ration was going to be!

But Flo and Betty, like everyone else, could rely for extra meat on the catching of rabbits which became only a little scarcer as time went on. In those days before myxomatosis they were seen by the hundred in local fields. But the local school kept over 200 rabbits in captivity and these provided much more meat on each rabbit.

They were looked after by the schoolchildren whose numbers were boosted by evacuee children from Plashet School in East Ham. Some were given to the mothers who came up from London on a Friday. Slaughtering mostly took place then so they could take a couple of rabbits back with them and the rest were sent home locally. Stan and Tony would often bring this 'superior' meat home for Flo, Betty and Harry as well as their Mum. The beauty for Harry and Flo was that 'school rabbits' didn't need skinning as this was done by the girls at school who then used the skins to make warm gloves for the winter.

The school also helped the war effort by involving the children in gardening - growing 'easy' crops like potatoes and marrows for school dinners, in school time, all part of the Dig For Victory campaign. Every afternoon a group of children would take the short walk up to the allotment, often unaccompanied, to spend the afternoon tending vegetables. Today, despite our renewed culture of eating fresh vegetables, much of the allotment land is not used for vegetable growing and is under grass.

As the war progressed, food became scarcer still. Civilian rations were very low. Everyone was allowed a small basic ration per week of tea, butter, milk and some tinned foods but Harry and the family had always grown a wide range of garden produce and along with the pig meat and Sid Richings' eggs and milk they did not suffer too badly, despite the monotony at certain times of the year. Pig killing now had to be done strictly under government licence and Batt Green held the licence for the village. One half of the carcass was supposed to be surrendered to the government and indeed some of it might have been! Domestic fires, particularly from 1941, had less and less coal to keep them alight so local woodlands became valuable as sources of kindling and extra fuel.

MINISTRY OF FOOD

RATION BOOK

OFFICIAL PAID

HOLDER'S NAME AND REGISTERED ADDRESS

Compare with your Identity Card and report any difference to your Food Office

DO NOT ALTER

Surname .... MANSELL

Other Names .... Harry

Address .... Longworth

ISSUED
JULY 1942

NAT. REG. NO.

If page is deposited retailer must write "YES" here.

MEAT
Name of Retailer............
Address............

BUTTER
Name of Retailer............ W. FREE
Address............ LONGWORTH, BERKS

BACON
Name of Retailer............ W. FREE
Address............ LONGWORTH, BERKS

SUGAR
Name of Retailer............ W. FREE
Address............ LONGWORTH, BERKS

CHEESE
Name of Retailer............ W. FREE
Address............ LONGWORTH, BERKS

EGGS W. FREE
FARINGDON RURAL
FOOD CONTROL Cancelled
COMMITTEE. PK

MILK Date of Birth if under 18

R.B.1 / 5
DO NOT fill in this space unless you deposit the page.
BUTTER
Surname MANSELL Initials HARRY
NAT. REG. No. DUJK 76 / 1

R.B.1 / 5
DO NOT fill in this space unless you deposit the page.
BACON
Surname MANSELL Initials H
NAT. REG. No. DUJK 76 / 1

R.B.1 / 5
DO NOT fill in this space unless you deposit the page.
SUGAR
Surname MANSELL Initials HARRY
NAT. REG. No. DUJK 76 / 1

R.B.1 / 5
DO NOT fill in this space unless you deposit the page.
CHEESE

R.B.1 / 5
DO NOT fill in this space unless you deposit the page.
FARINGDON RURAL FOOD CONTROL COMMITTEE PK
EGGS

R.B.1 / 5
DO NOT fill in this space unless you deposit the page.
TEA
Holder's MANSELL Initials HARRY

97

CLOTHING CARD
Ration Period to 31 May, 1942

Serial Number **CC 549003**

NUMBER OF COUPONS REQUIRED

Men and Boys	Adults	Children
Unlined mackintosh or cape	9	7
Other mackintoshes, raincoat, overcoat	16	11
Coat, jacket, blazer and like garments	13	8
Waistcoat, pull-over, cardigan, jersey	5	3
Trousers (other than fustian or corduroy)	8	6
Fustian or corduroy trousers	5	5
Shorts	5	3
Overalls, dungarees and like garments	6	4
Dressing-gown, bathing-gown, or pair of pyjamas	8	6
Shirt, combinations—woollen	8	6
Shirt, combinations—other material	5	4
Pants, vest, bathing costume, child's blouse	4	2
Pair of socks or stockings	3	1
Collar, tie, or two handkerchiefs	1	1
Scarf, pair of gloves or mittens	2	2
Pair of slippers or goloshes	4	2
Pair of boots or shoes	7	3
Pair of leggings, gaiters or spats	3	2

Women and Girls	Adults	Children
Coat, raincoat, lined mackintosh	14	11
Jacket, short coat	11	8
Dress, gown, frock—woollen	11	8
Dress, gown, frock—other material	7	5
Gym, tunic, girl's skirt with bodice	8	6
Blouse, sports shirt, cardigan, jumper	5	3
Skirt, divided skirt	7	5
Overalls, dungarees and like garments	6	4
Apron, pinafore	3	2
Pyjamas	8	6
Nightdress	6	5
Petticoat, slip, combinations, cami-knickers	4	3
Other undergarments, including corsets	3	2
Pair of stockings	2	1
Pair of socks, collar, tie, or two handkerchiefs	1	1
Scarf, pair of gloves or mittens, muff	2	2
Pair of slippers, boots or shoes	5	3

Cloth.—Coupons needed per yard depend on the width, for example, a yard of woollen cloth 36 ins. wide requires 3 coupons and cotton or other cloth 2 coupons.

Harry could no longer use his lorry for his business with wartime restrictions on petrol and on building materials in force and, with the likelihood of Reg and Fred and other employees required for active service, his business soon stopped for the duration. Even after the war having to use petrol coupons for his lorry meant that trading was more difficult. His lorry, however, as one of the few motorised vehicles in the village at the time did sterling service wherever required for the war effort.

The older generation.

Harry and Flo Mansell above left. Harry Mansell with Florrie Richings (wife of Albert Richings).

Flo Mansell with her sister-in-law, Florrie Richings. Keith Luckett at the wheel.

Harry joins the Home Guard

The first months of the war saw the setting up in Longworth of the Local Defence Volunteers under Colonel Walton of Longworth Manor. It later became the huge civilian army known as the Home Guard which militarised civilians in case of a last stand against the enemy. This was new! The threat of invasion was very real. The older men of Harry Mansell's extended family, those over forty, including Harry himself, his brother-in-law Sid Richings and Flo's cousin Nolan Tubb, enrolled.

Harry in uniform

Longworth Home Guard's basic role was to protect the district and stand ready for action if required. Sid, not a healthy man, didn't last beyond the early stages of the LDVs, however. Harry's only uniform at the beginning was an armband (think early editions of Dad's Army!), but as time went on he wore combat uniform - a khaki battledress with a rifle, but no ammunition. There were strict rules about what ammunition, if any, they could carry with them at any given time. Harry's nephews Tony and Stan Gutteridge recalled their Uncle Harry saying, "If a 'Jerry' lands in that field I've got to go up to him and say, 'Just wait a minute while I nip over there and get my ammunition and I'll come back and arrest you'." Then Tony and Stan would ask, "Will you do that Uncle Harry?" "No I bloody shan't – I'll take my twelve bore." But Harry Mansell never fired his rifle!

Harry and Nolan and the other members of the Home Guard would rendezvous at Home Farm at least in the early days of the war and then march down to Lamb Pit Quarry where they would take part in shooting and bayonet practice. The training was not just physical, it also took the form of many hours a week in a long series of 'essential' lectures and courses at the Village Institute. Local training and theory sessions were beefed up with lectures and courses in Faringdon. Harry and his platoon learnt the theory and practice of communications, first aid, map reading, field craft, basic outdoor survival techniques and how to set booby-traps, ambush the enemy, destroy their machines and artillery and, not least, hand-to-hand combat. Harry took his turn patrolling the streets at night to ensure that nothing untoward was happening and that no strangers could pass or hide. As the nearest siren was at Faringdon they had to rely on men patrolling the Faringdon Road as well as the few telephones in the village to keep them informed of any significant news.

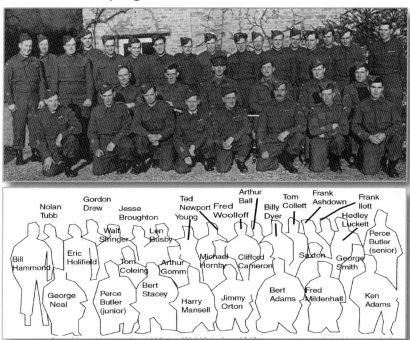

Home Guard: Longworth & Hinton Waldrist, circa 1942.

British Armed Forces were billeted at Longworth House in Lodge Lane, Longworth Manor and at Home Farm as well as in ordinary homes. Many households, like Flo Mansell's, took in the soldiers' washing and even sold strawberries and other fresh fruit to them. Houses of all sizes took in evacuees. Parts of the big houses and fields, including most of Home Farm's top field, were commandeered for use by the soldiers for the duration of the war. Home Farm was used as a depot for the Home Guards and the equipment and ammunition they used were stored there.

Nigel Drew described how The Honourable Artillery Company (HAC) who had their Longworth base at Home Farm had an ack-ack gun (short for anti-aircraft artillery) which was kept in a corner by the hedge close to his childhood home in the centre of the village, where it was considered to be safe from tampering and of most use in the event of invasion. A little while after the HAC left, the US Army moved in and, whilst billeted in the village, they began the task of receiving and unpacking aircraft parts at Home Farm for onward transit to Kingston Bagpuize aerodrome. The Home Guard helped when needed. Nigel reported that servicemen, 'spread copious amounts of flintstone from the boundary of the Square back to the farmhouse to provide a significantly sized hardstanding for the many lorries bearing heavy imports of aircraft pieces and machinery.'

The hedge between the Home Farm field and Yew Tree Cottage where young Nigel lived was drastically cut back and the wall was flattened so he soon found that to his delight he became great friends with the 'Yanks' next door. Harry Mansell's nephews were similarly happy to see a range of extraordinary machines and equipment, such as artillery, graders, large bulldozers, caterpillar

102

tractors, Bailey bridges, pontoons and searchlights arrive in and around the village. The ack-ack gun was never fired in anger. The Home Guard was wound down at the end of 1944.

Troops abound

There were troops and equipment everywhere. At first the troops were all British but later the Americans came too – mostly engineers and their masses of equipment. The Home Guard supported the soldiers, ensuring that supplies and equipment, particularly the large mounds of equipment under tarpaulins all along the roadsides out of the village, were safe and ready. They checked that nothing was going missing – but local children had an eye to earning the odd copper or two by purloining some bits and pieces – and cordite! Young local lads, like Harry's nephews, Stan and Tony, and friends such as Ray Dunsdon, had a great deal to say about the war in their various conversations years later. Several stories were rehearsed about when the guard hut by the gate into the Home Farm paddock was used for housing recalcitrant prisoners of war. But it was not all fun for the children – some of them reported being upset when their parents and other grown-ups heard the hum of planes overhead and acted warily.

There were many hair-raising events. One occurred when Flo Mansell's sister, Hilda Gutteridge, was living with her three children in Little London, across the road from Roadside Farm (now Fallowfields Hotel). One day, whilst the children were at home, Hilda was out delivering papers for Drayton's shop in Southmoor, when she saw a plane, apparently out of control and trailing smoke, losing height and heading straight for her home at Little London. Seemingly, at the last minute, an explosion on the plane lifted it across the road where it crashed in Roadside Farm land.

Hilda's son Tony reported, "Our Mum thought it was going to land on our house but then she remarked to a friend, 'Oh no, it's missed it', and carried on delivering papers!" This account could be said to illustrate the 'carry on regardless' spirit of the period.

Hilda Gutteridge's children, Tony, Marina and Stan at the time when they were living in Little London.

Tony and his brother Stan collected bits of perspex, balsa and plywood from the crash site and made carved mementoes out of them.

Farming in difficult times

As time went on, Tony Slade of Home Farm employed anyone he could to work the land and tend pigs, sheep and market gardening crops. Many village fields had been dug up for the 'Dig For Victory' campaign which was in full swing for growing vegetables. With many local men away on active service, Tony and other farmers scoured local villages as far away as Bampton and Stanford in the Vale for women to work on the land. Tony Slade had a poor opinion of Land Girls but valued the German and Italian prisoners of war. After years of working the land all through the war and in the years afterwards he improved growing conditions on much of the light sandy soil.

Happily he found the right combination of intensive pig-rearing and market gardening and his Welsh White pigs later won many prizes. An article in Farmer's Weekly in the 1950s said that, 'Mr Slade was making a profit of over £4,000 a year and he is of course a major employer in the village, and has bought and built new houses for his employees.' Tony Slade, with Ken and Gordon Maclean, was responsible for the construction of the original Log Cabin in Southmoor so that local produce could be sold more readily to local people.

Betty's war work

Flo was not very well during much of the war and depended on Betty who found local work after she left school. Betty worked at Free's shop – the Post Office and general stores in The Square. As virtual housekeeper for three men and with a mother who was not well, spending time queuing for food and preparing nourishing meals with no refrigerator or other 'mod cons', Betty would already have been kept rather busy. But as a single woman she was required to help the war effort in some way. So after she left Free's she cycled each day to a fifteen-acre site secreted in the dark, dense conifer woodland of Tubney Woods where Bofors – double-barrelled anti-aircraft guns - were manufactured. This is known in local circles as 'The Hush Hush Factory in the Woods', but its formal name was the Nuffield Mechanisation and Aero Shadow Factory.

Lord Nuffield had already set up a plant in Coventry in 1938 feeling that Britain was badly prepared to withstand aerial bombardment – when a direct hit by the German air force early in the war meant that a more remote site was required urgently. The Tubney site opened in 1940. Once a bus was laid on through local villages more and more people could come to work at the site. Ray Dunsdon's father, whose wife was a cousin of Flo Mansell, was invalided out of the First World War but was able to work at the site, on light duties. He took the bus which started picking up along the route from Faringdon once the company was in full swing.

Others working there from further afield were at first provided with accommodation in sheds and public houses in local villages such as Appleton before a series of prefabs in the area now known as The Ride just north of the factory site nearer the Faringdon Road, were erected. The Tubney factory shut down after the war and remained forgotten and increasingly derelict until the early 1990s. The site is now the location of 'Oxford Instruments'.

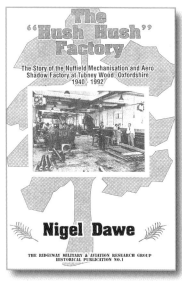

For further details of the wartime 'Hush Hush Factory' read Nigel Dawe's booklet on the subject.

Fred goes to war

Neither Fred nor Reg were called up at the very beginning of the war and both were said to be disappointed as both were keen to do their bit. As Reg was the older of the two brothers their expectation was that he would be called up first. But late in 1939 Fred was called up and aged nearly 21, he went off for training - a keen young recruit ready to take part. But Fred's entry into the theatre of war was delayed when he became a victim of a car accident in Bournemouth. He was run over in the dark by an Army Medical Officer's car during a pre-training session and his leg was broken. Unhappily, he spent his 21st birthday in hospital. Fred's response later was robust:

"You know who the country-folk are because they can find their way around in the dark, townsfolk are used to street lights!"

If Fred had known what was in store for him in the near future he may well have wished for an even longer period of convalescence!

Fred, a fully qualified carpenter with a bent for machines, in 1942 went into the Royal Engineers who were responsible for the servicing, maintenance and inspection of all equipment. Only one disadvantage marred his ability to fulfil his full potential - he was chronically car sick!

Fred in army uniform and wearing a Universal Pattern Field Service Cap (a Glengarry), rapidly abandoned by the British Army when serving in the searing sun of India.

Fred's war was spent in the 2nd Division of the Fourteenth Army - the 'Forgotten Army' - far away from the European theatres of war and off the radar of the media.

Left: Fred, in more appropriate headgear for the Indo-Burmese frontier.
Right: Writing home in February 1943, from somewhere in the Burma/North-East India theatre. Fred makes light of his conditions.

Photo (enlarged) with Fred (front left) with "a few of the lads" outside their tent in the jungle, 1943.

Sapper Mansell. F.G, 2008693
5th Field Coy. R.E.
Section 3.
c/o Army Base Post Office
India.

14/2/43

Dear Mum & all,

Just a few lines hoping you are all quite well as this leaves me the same at present. We are still in the jungle living in tents but as most of us have made beds for ourselves out of bamboo it is not too bad at all. You will find a photo in this letter of a few of the lads taken outside our tent and you can see for yourself we do not look too bad. We had them printed small as they are better for posting this size but if you want it should be easy to get an enlargement of it. Des said in his last letter that his mother has got a apple pie waiting for when I get back and it seems to me that if things keep moving as fast as they are at present it may not be so long before I am eating it. Well I think I will have to close now so I'll say cheerio,

Your loving son
Fred.

Camp
February
1943.

North-west Burma saw vicious fighting with attack and counter-attack in a struggle to control the area from the encroaching Japanese, who threatened to capture the vitally strategic route through the Naga Hills of Assam to the major British supply base at Dimapur and Imphal. This culminated in a major Japanese attack on what became known as the Battle of Kohima Ridge which began on 4th April 1944.

The 2nd Division of the Fourteenth Army arrived on the scene on April 14th and the Division fought the Japanese in a desperately savage and very bloody battle in these malaria-infested hill slopes where heavy rain, mud, leeches, ticks and huge logistical problems were made even worse by the mix of languages and mis-understandings among the participants and among those responsible for bringing in fresh supplies of food and weaponry. What a surreal, nerve-shredding experience and all the time men desperate for rest and respite.

British and Indian troops fought off the Japanese with periods of intense close-quarter fighting. It must have been a total nightmare – corpses rotting and men wilting in the searing temperatures. However, by 22nd June, the Japanese were in full retreat but at a cost of over 4,000 allied lives in this battle alone.

But this was to be the turning point in the war. This battle crushed the final Japanese bid to invade India. There then began the long thrust pushing the Japanese southwards back through Burma. Mandalay fell on 19th March 1945 and by 3rd May Rangoon was in allied hands. Japan did not finally concede defeat until August 1945.

How disorienting was it to sit in these tropical hills writing postcards and letters home in the weeks after the battle of Kohima? Fred must have worried about Reg and how he was getting on. How much did he know about what was going on in Europe? Fred was not repatriated for many, many months after Kohima. After the battle, Fred found himself in a platoon of the Fifth Field Company of the Fourth Brigade of the Royal Engineers preparing to mop up the aftermath of battle and make good some of the destruction of property, but the fast-growing jungle vegetation soon hid much of the war-scarred territory.

The Division set about building a memorial in the cemetery for the war dead of Kohima where so many of their less fortunate fellow servicemen perished. Fred used the skills of his building trade to great effect but the local stone was particularly hard and unforgiving and a chisel could be reduced in length by an inch each day and so specialist stone workers were shipped in to help. Fred worked on a large inscribed monolith linked to two curved walls which later bore the names of the fallen. It stands at Kohima, at the point where there was the hardest fighting, set among a number of other memorials to the fallen.

Right: Unveiling the War Memorial of the 2nd Division of the Fourteenth Army, at Kohima. All regiments of the division were represented at the ceremony. The illustrations are from the SEAC (South East Asia Command) Newspaper of 19th and 22nd Nov 1944.

Fred would not return home until many weeks after the Victory over Japan (VJ) Day festivities back in Europe. His mother, Flo, very ill by now, was hanging on hoping to see him safely home to ensure the future comfort of the rest of the family, especially Reg whose own wartime experience had been very grim.

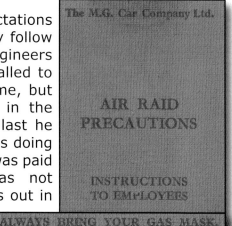

SECOND DIVISION HONOURS ITS DEAD

When you go home
Tell them of us and say,
For your tomorrow
We gave our today

TWO HUNDRED NAGAS BROUGHT THE MEMORIAL STONE FROM THE HILLS AND PLACED IT IN POSITION. THIS WAS THEIR TRIBUTE TO THE FALLEN

The caption reads: Two hundred Nagas brought the memorial stone from the hills and placed it in position. This was their tribute to the fallen.

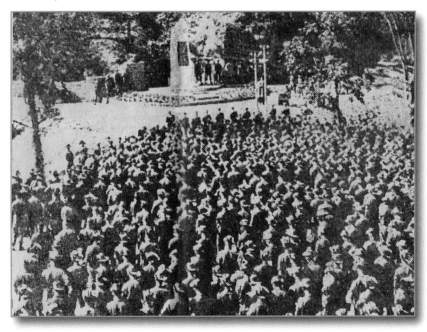

The Home Secretary presents his compliments and has the honour to transmit the enclosed Defence Medal which has been awarded in recognition of service during the war of 1939-45.

The Under-Secretary of State for Defence (Armed Forces) presents his compliments and by Command of the Defence Council has the honour to transmit the enclosed Awards granted for service during the war of 1939—45

Mansell awards, medals and insignia from World War Two (1939 - 1945).

Reg's War – disappointment and horror

Reg Mansell awaits the war. His car was a Singer.

Reg was extremely disappointed that he was not was called up first, before his younger brother Fred. He began to think he would never go to war despite conscription which, in 1939, applied to all non-exempt men aged 18-41 years. However, the younger men were usually chosen first. The family business had been wound up for the duration of the war and Reg had to find work. He went to the MG works in Abingdon eight miles away. It was unusual for anyone who lived in Longworth to work far outside Longworth before the Second World War – most of Longworth's workforce at that time still worked in or very close to Longworth parish – and nearly all of those people were employed on the farms.

Now things began to change and groups of workers, large and small, could be seen strung out like beads along the roads around the village heading for work at Tubney or in neighbouring towns like Abingdon. It took the war and its aftermath to bring on the sea-change that meant most workers were eventually employed outside the village, enjoying much improved transport, much better wages, and good working conditions.

The MG works, founded at Abingdon in 1929, had to cease production of cars in 1939 and take up high volume production of weaponry and aircraft parts. It was here that Reg and many others from villages such as Longworth went in that year on a short contract when many new workers were required. MG not only replaced those men who had been called up but took on hundreds of new workers, too old or too young to go to war, and 300 women too. MG went into war production mode involving a massive increase in output compared with the days of car manufacture. The factory was split up into five different sections making and assembling new tanks, overhauling old tanks, making aircraft engine parts and manufacturing a great range of other components and spares.

Reg still had high expectations that he would eventually follow Fred into the Royal Engineers and that he would be called to active service at any time, but he was happy working in the tank section at MG. At last he felt really useful – he was doing something he liked and was paid relatively well and was not working on building sites out in the countryside in all weathers. However, with no Abingdon bus he would cycle to and fro in all seasons.

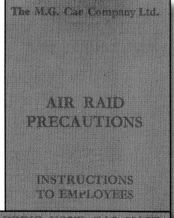

The M.G. Car Company Ltd.

AIR RAID
PRECAUTIONS

INSTRUCTIONS
TO EMPLOYEES

ALWAYS BRING YOUR GAS MASK.

Always co-operate with the Shelter Marshals, Wardens and other Volunteer Services by obeying their orders willingly and quietly.

In the pocket of his work overalls Reg kept, for many years after the war, a small, much-thumbed and oil-stained booklet, a copy of MG Works News (see overleaf). He also kept a homily put together by the management entitled 'The Need for Individual Responsibility', with quotations from speeches given by HM The King, Winston Churchill and others. Also found amongst Reg's belongings was an MG Air Raid Precautions card (see below).

Read these instructions carefully and retain this card for reference.

Name ...... *R. W. MANSELL* ......

Clock No. ...... *7139 / 1181* ......

Department ...... *TEMPEST.* ......

Home Address ...... *Church Rd.* ......
...... *Longworth* ......
...... *Abingdon* ......
...... *Berks.* ......

Your Shelter is No. ...... *24* ......

YOUR SHELTER MARSHAL IS :

MR. ...... *A. Williams.* ......

MARSHALS
It is the duty of Marshals and their Deputies to ensure as far as possible that everybody in his/her Shop or Department has taken cover when the " Take Shelter " signal has been sounded.

GENERAL
In order to ensure the maximum amount of security possible for employees, a system of ROOF WATCHERS and INTERNAL WARNINGS has been adopted and is in operation at these Works.
Employees joining the Company or transferring to another Department of the Company will immediately report to the Shelter Marshal of that Department.

" ALERT " CAUTIONARY SIGNAL
The presence of enemy aircraft in the area will be indicated by the illumination of single RED LIGHTS throughout the Factory.
When these lights are burning, employees may at their option take shelter, but the Management recommends, having in mind the purpose of the scheme, that employees continue at work until they receive the " Take Shelter " signal from the Spotters.

" TAKE SHELTER " SIGNAL
The " TAKE SHELTER " signal will consist of a succession of short blasts on the Klaxons.
Employees should remain in their Shelters until they receive the " ALL CLEAR " signal:
ONE continuous blast of 30 seconds on the Klaxons.

In the event of an Air Raid developing before shelter is reached, advantage should be taken of any cover immediately at hand. LIE DOWN and cover your head with your arms.
Should the " Take Shelter " signal be sounded when away from your Shop or Department, evacuate with the Shop or Department you are in.
When the " All Clear " is sounded employees should then return to their Shops and Departments without delay and be ready to repeat the procedure if and when necessary.

Air Raid Precautions. Detailed instructions to MG employees.

From the MG WORKS NEWS NO 2 1941

As everyone is aware, the *War Effort Award* is a purely voluntary contribution made by the Management to certain employees in recognition of any merit or effort that it is considered should be rewarded. As promised, the details have now been worked out to simplify the scope of the Award, by making everyone - whether hourly paid or weekly paid - eligible, with the sole exception of operatives already on piece-work.

This War Effort Award will bear some relation to the actual output of the factory in a simple way which everyone can understand, and will be additional to any War Effort already being paid. A simple chart will be prominently displayed in each section of the factory, and from this will be seen that the War Effort Award, to be distributed each week by the Management, depends upon the total number of hours booked by that Department in relation to the number of units of output.

With regard to piece-work operatives . . . . they will be paid on the average *War Effort Award* of the productive sections. Office Staff will also participate to the extent of 50% of the *War Effort Award* awarded.

Signed *Cecil Kimber*

.

Cecil Kimber was the founding leader of MG Abingdon but was dismissed in 1941 shortly after this notice was written. He tragically died in a railway accident not long after the war.

These months at MG were among the happiest of Reg's working life but his life was soon to take an abrupt turn and he was to be desperately unlucky.

Reg's call to war did not come until the summer of 1943. His war service record shows that he was classified medically fit - 'A1' - in June 1943. He was a general builder who had become an excellent plasterer - a skilled workman. He had spent long enjoyable hours in his workshop in Butts Lane (the garage they had managed to cobble together at Number 2 Butts Lane) working on a lathe, building a steam engine. Add to this his experience at the MG works in Abingdon and he fondly imagined that he would follow his brother into the Royal Engineers. He was said to have been sorely disappointed to be in training as 'a sapper in the pioneers with its dependence on hard physical work'. As Stan Gutteridge remarked, 'He was plonked in a pioneer regiment when he would much rather have been in the Royal Engineers like his brother.' His war service card however shows that he did receive a very comprehensive training for the Royal Fusiliers.

Whilst under training in September 1943.
Reg Mansell is in the second row, second from the left.

119

Reg, like his brother and father, was of short stature – five foot six inches and with hazel eyes, brown hair and a fresh complexion. He was always considered to be 'a very good-looking kind of chap' in Longworth. When he signed on he described himself as a builder's foreman. He was provided with army standard issue clothing: nine battledress blouses and trousers; five denim blouses and trousers, one cap, boots, three pairs of socks, an Angola shirt, woollen vests; woollen drawers and three short cellular drawers and a grey coat. He trained first at Colchester and then with the 7th Battalion, the Oxfordshire and Buckinghamshire Light Infantry Brigade, based at Cowley Military Barracks where he undertook various courses and training as a fusilier.

He was taught the use of light weaponry - rifles and Bren guns (light machine guns), he threw hand grenades and fired mortars and was fired over by the artillery. He also underwent tests for mustard gas in gas chambers and also administered as drops to test his sensitivity. On one intensive training course he had to build up his fitness to run long distances carrying a backpack: he could run ten miles in two hours. He sent a letter home whilst training in Colchester but this is the only correspondence from him that has survived. He showed a real longing for the comforts of home and fresh food! By January 1944, his training complete, and after repeated inoculations against typhoid and fourteen days embarkation leave he was ready for the theatre of war.

Reg, now in the Royal Fusiliers, went to Italy as part of Operation Shingle and the resulting long Battle of Anzio, 35 miles south of Rome. Though ultimately successful for the Allies the campaign in North Italy was going badly. The Battle lasted from January to the end of May 1944 by which time Reg was one of the 42,000 casualties on the Allies side - 7,000 of these were killed. At home his family received a telegram dated 4th March with the news that he had been 'wounded on 17th February 1944 in the Central Mediterranean Theatre of War'. More worryingly still this was followed two days later by an official letter with the dreadful news that he was 'dangerously ill at a hospital in the Central Mediterranean Theatre of War. From shot wound thigh' (see letter overleaf).

Reg received gunshot wounds to both thighs and widespread shrapnel injuries too within two hours of his first real action in battle on 17th February 1944. However, grimly, in some ways Reg was lucky! Most of his close comrades on that day were killed! But, horrifically, his life was further endangered because he then spent many hours, a whole night, hanging in a thorn bush during a fire-fight, bleeding and in great pain, before enemy snipers close by could be gunned down; after which, mercifully, Reg was lifted out of the thorn bush and he and all the wounded were given first aid and the dead gathered up. Only then was Reg transported to hospital locally before being shipped back to Cowley Road Hospital in Oxford where he convalesced for many months. His injuries put him out of the war.

A commonwealth grave in Anzio stands as a memorial to those from Reg's regiment and other regiments who lost their lives. Like his father, Reg was badly affected for the rest of his life by his wartime injuries. He received an army pension based on the assessment that he was 30% disabled - unable to father children and having significant muscular damage to his legs. He was also said to be 'unable to walk backwards', which was more disabling for a builder than might be supposed, but apparently he was a very good dancer! His experience of war was briefer by far than Fred's (or his father's) – just one year and 278 days service in all – his effective discharge was 16th January 1945 when his medical classification was 'E'.

No. _Ca/OBLI/10208_

(If replying please quote above No.)

Army Form B. 104—80

Infantry Record Office,

Warwick Station

6th March, 19 _44_.

S̶i̶r̶, Madam,

I regret to have to inform you that a report has this day been received from the War Office to the effect that (No.) _14624226_

(Rank) _Pte_ (Name) _MANSELL, R.W.L._

(Regiment) OXF. & BUCKS. L. I. _20 Feb._ is dangerously ill at _a hospital in the Central Mediterranean_ suffering _Theatre of War._ from _Shot wound thigh._ _Battle casualty_

I am at the same time to express the sympathy and regret of the Army Council.

Any further information received at this office as to his condition or progress will be at once notified to you.

I am,

S̶i̶r̶, Madam,

Your obedient Servant,

John May _for_ _W/Col._

Officer in charge of Records.

Wt.30259/1267. 500M. 9/39. KJL/8817. Gp.698/3. Forms/B104—80/5.

122

6. The Return

The soldiers' return

red Mansell was awarded the Burma Star for his service in the Burmese war theatre (see page 114). This was a prestigious award which he greatly valued. He regularly attended the annual reunions of the Faringdon & District Branch of the Burma Star Association founded in 1951 – which usually took the form of an annual dinner dance at Buckland Memorial Hall.

Their Guests of Honour included in 1975 the son of the well-known leader of the Burma Campaign, the second Viscount Slim. The subscriptions paid by the members of the Association contributed towards welfare work for veterans of the Burma Campaign. Both Fred and Reg were closely involved with the British Legion (later becoming The Royal British Legion), founded in 1921 when it brought together the four national organisations of ex-servicemen established just after the First World War. They paid their subscriptions for the rest of their lives in support of those who had been to war and their families.

Fred Gutteridge, Fred and Reg Mansell's uncle, who returned from active service in the Navy in 1945, found that family life was not all a bed of roses – his three children had had an amazing amount of freedom during the war, with no father around and their mother Hilda busy with different jobs to help make ends meet, they were to find it very difficult to adapt on his return.

Fred was virtually a complete stranger to them. Their mother Hilda, like other women left behind by their husbands would have found it very strange too to have a grown man in the family again. But they both got on with

123

life with their three children and later Hilda was able to pick up her teaching career again at Buckland School. But, almost as bad, Fred was aghast at the long term privations of his family. He had been shielded from the worst of the frugality of wartime food and its constant shortages suffered by those left at home. Most serving men had had a high calorie diet served up in sufficient quantity as a priority. Matters would get worse before the food supply eased again, long after the war when rationing tapered off. Fred's brother never did return home. He fought in Palestine. After seven years out there, on the onset of the war he had got married but was killed in France less than two weeks later.

Sadly picking up the pieces

At the Mansell home in Church Road, Fred's long absence on the India-Burma front, months after the war ended, had added to the angst suffered by a family struggling to cope with Flo in declining health. The years of worry had been followed by the anxiety attendant on Reg's dreadful injuries, and the difficulties of visiting him during his long hospital stay in Cowley Road Hospital on the other side of Oxford. Flo was, according to her nephew Stan, keen to 'hang on' in time to see Fred return in late autumn 1945.

She lived to see Reg back home and making a slow improvement as his wounds healed. She had been upset that Reg might never work again, but happily she was reassured that Fred would look after him and it was clear that Reg was slowly making at least a partial recovery from his injuries. Flo sadly died on 12th January 1946 aged 54 after nearly 32 years of marriage to Harry, and was buried in Longworth churchyard.

One of the last pictures of Flo and Harry together.

Flo had died before the official Welcome Home party in 1946 was organised. Each village and township in Britain held a Victory Day party for the servicemen and women who by the early summer would be mostly back home. Earlier celebrations had been held for VE (Victory in Europe) Day and VJ (Victory over Japan) Days. Harry was on the Village Institute committee which was making plans for Longworth's party in the summer of 1946. The Welcome Home involved a parade of all those from the services, starting at 'Billy Bright's solid wooden gates' (still called that even though Billy had gone to Charney Bassett to live and no longer rented the fields behind the gates) on the Square in Longworth, facing the Post Office.

The Victory Day Parade (1946) went round the village ending at the Village Institute for a 'lavish lunch' at the invitation of the organising committee. At least that was the idea; the reality was rabbit stew! Everyone was told where to sit down to eat but Harry found himself staring at a plate with the head of a rabbit on it and could not face it. It is said that he 'moved up a place' to avoid the head. And who could blame him! Rationing was bringing more privation than ever and was making catering more and more difficult - no one had party food to share, even for the Welcome Home party.

Harry and his sons and daughter pulled together as Reg regained some of his health and fitness. The building trades started back to work and Fred and Harry threw themselves into making a living in Longworth. Harry over the years had done a great deal of work at Longworth Manor – sometimes major works and later making cement moulds to manufacture ornate tops for the stone gate posts he built. He diversified as he grew older and did less heavy work; constructing bird baths and small statues and garden ornaments as well as headstones for local graves.

There were no thoughts of marriage, at least on the two brothers' behalf. Betty would marry Edgar Keith Luckett in October 1948 but she would not go far away. Their two children are later seen in many a photograph chatting with Fred. Reg's war wounds meant he could never have children and the two brothers gave every impression of being confirmed bachelors, especially after Fred had promised his mother that he would always look after his elder brother. Betty, as seemed right and proper in those days, was housekeeper for them all.

Brothers and sisters

Hilda and Fred had lived at Little London since 1931 but it was rather a tight fit in her rundown cottage - it felt rather small and uncomfortable after their second son, Tony, and daughter Marina came along - even after Sid and Cis and their children moved out! In 1949 they moved to Windrush, the vacant and much bigger and better appointed house next door, at the invitation of the owner Mr Paine. He must have felt rather sorry for them all, but when he wanted to marry in 1953 and move back in they had to leave. Hilda's brother, Sid, had on her behalf, bought at auction both the Wickham Cottages on Hinton Road, for about £800. However, the sitting tenants there remained where they were and this meant Hilda would not be able to move in. She had to move to a house in Faringdon with her children. Fred found a very cheap bungalow for them to buy in Sutton Courtenay but Hilda could not bring herself to move so far from Longworth. She never did live back in Longworth, however, and Hilda and Fred ended their days at Novi Dom on Faringdon Road in Southmoor.

Flo's other sister Agnes had married Frank Patrick in the early 1930s and worked at a car factory in Coventry. During the blitz on Coventry they had their house roof blown off during a bombing raid whilst they cowered inside. They then moved to Cowley to do war work. They had no children. Flo's brother Will, who served in the Great War was, of course, too old for the second war. A builder before the war he had married Ethel Weston in 1938 and moved to Gozzard's Ford near Abingdon but he died before the end of the war, in 1942, aged only 46. They also had no children.

As the war came to an end, the health of Flo's other brother Sid was very poor, he gave up his cows and sold his retail milk-round to Fred Broughton of Glen Farm, and the Broughton family continued it for many years. Sid died aged fifty in 1950, the same year Harry lost his brother Ivo. Sid left five very young children – Peter, Fay, Susan, Mary and Kathleen. His widow, Cis, struggled to bring in enough to raise the family and as their daughter Mary Belcher said, 'It was horrendous in those days. Mum used to work on the land during the day and do all sorts of work at the New Inn as a barmaid in the evening.' Eventually Cis married Leslie Hacker and moved from Barn Ground cottages to Southmoor where they lived in the old Post Office at the end of School Lane. She died in 1996.

The Butts

After the war, endeavouring to pick up the threads of work again and keep busy after Flo's death, Harry negotiated the purchase of the property he had set his heart on when he had first moved into the rented cottage in Church Road. Harry was determined to move on and leave the rented property behind to live in his own home and he once again made plans.

The property in Butts Lane had served as a builder's yard and the old lean-to had been improved and had already become Reg's workshop before the war, vying for space with the family's lorry. Soon they would get permission to do up the house and move in.

No 2, Butts Lane. The Mansell's new home in 1947.

Most householders in those days rented their homes throughout their lives, but the purchase of a derelict property by those able to carry out the labour themselves at this time would make good sense, and with business slow after the war they could spend time refurbishing the property – once Fred was back from Burma.

Harry finally bought the title deed of Number 2 Butts Lane in 1947 and in May that year they were given permission by the Ministry of Works to go ahead with the completion of the property - on condition they spent no more than £600 on it and did not put it up for sale at more than £1200 or let it out without a formal determination of its maximum rentable value. But they were going to live in it themselves so none of that mattered.

They finished the work which they had started before the war - putting it into a habitable state and turning a once derelict near ruin into a good 'spacious' home. Interestingly it was about this time that Butts Lane officially became Rectory Lane. Previously the lane was known to different people by different names! Just as Church Lane and Church Road seemed to be used contemporaneously by some locals! Harry, nevertheless, called their new home The Butts.

Fred and Harry, with the otherwise under-employed men in the resurrected H. Mansell business, refurbished the outer fabric, re-roofed the house with Stonesfield slate and put in new windows. They had already saved the house from certain ruin but The Butts was now a lovely cottage. Harry, Fred, Reg and Betty and, a little later, her new husband Keith Luckett all moved in in 1948.

Harry escorting Betty to her wedding.

During the war Keith Luckett had served in the RAF driving crash tenders and cranes in the desert in Africa. After the war he worked at AERE Harwell driving cranes and buses until his retirement years later.

Keith had inherited a small cottage (see above), only two doors away, and when it was ready Betty would still be on hand to help the three men when necessary. The Lucketts later had a motorised fish and chip van and in the early days they toured the local villages many evenings a week, selling the only fast food available in those days. The locals queued up eagerly awaiting a hot meal. Later, the van, now less roadworthy, sold fish and chips from 'over the garden wall'. The van remained in the garden long after it had served any useful purpose.

The business of H. Mansell slowly began to pick up once The Butts was ready for them to move into. But soon Harry retired as his health deteriorated and Fred took over as proprietor.

Fred takes over as proprietor of the business.

Fred worked hard to build up a workforce and a clientele as building regulations relaxed. He employed local lads including Bernard and Ray Dunsdon, Norman Carter, Gerald Parsons, Cyril Couling and Paul Hubbard, some of whom had just left school, and now that he was well enough Reg joined in too.

They worked on many a building in and around Longworth and later even laid sewage pipes when the time came for the village to have mains sewerage. They worked extensively on the Lamb & Flag, Home Farm, the chimney at Haugh House, the summer-house in the corner of Longworth Manor garden, a stone wall at the Royal Oak on Appleton Road, the porch on Lincoln Lodge and a virtual rebuild of the Post Office, on the square in Longworth in the 1960s, among many other properties in the area. The Post Office took a very long time to do and the owner was getting impatient but a good job could not be hurried. Obviously this was not held against them as they were later asked to build the retirement home for the Frees – in the Free's own back garden – which now, like so many of Longworth's stone cottages and other homes, has been massively enlarged.

Many other properties such as the barn at the Old Rectory also had work done by the Mansell family – in particular the Stonesfield slate roof. They also built the swimming pool at New House just outside Southmoor on Hanney Road.

The Post Office and Store in Longworth Square, looking towards Tuck's Lane.

133

The Store and Post Office in Longworth Square before and after the rebuilding. Below: Further work in progress.

Mansell and Dunsdon working on demolition.

H. Mansell, Building Contractor. Standing left to right: Fred Mansell, Gerald Parsons, Paul Hubbard and Reg Mansell. On the truck, Ray Dunsdon

Meanwhile, Reg and Fred took to tinkering with their motorbikes, running them up and down Butts Lane in any free time they had – mostly at the weekend and on summer evenings, and this drew a large audience. Their cousin Tony Gutteridge remembered:

"For years when the Mansells were down Butt's Lane (as I knew it) lots of the village boys and some of the village girls used to meet down there on Sunday mornings. Fred and Reg used to have their motorbikes out. If anybody we didn't know came round – 'Whose old boy be you then?' If they could say something like, 'Oh, I'm Perce Butler's youngest.' We would say 'Oh, that's all right then.' All these villages have grown so much, it's not just Longworth. We were very clannish. We could fight amongst ourselves but if anyone fought us we all fought together against them. When I was a boy you needed to be very brave to be a Longworth boy and walk through Hinton and Kingston on your own."

Longworth Youth getting around on wheels. Bernard Dunsdon (right). Below: Norman Carter.

136

Death of Harry

Harry Mansell died in January 1953, aged 63, at Vale House in Botley. Harry would have considered himself an ordinary working man from an ordinary line of builders, masons and plasterers just doing their best. But he lived an extraordinary life by modern standards – most of his generation did. He lived at a time when he could not make choices of his own – and nor could his sons.

He served his country well, going to war when required and overcoming reverses, separations and dreadful memories of trench warfare from his First World War experiences. He had had to pick up his trade twice when war intervened and see both his sons go off to war. But he never made a fuss despite having the misfortune to be caught up in two world wars, just like so many other war veterans of his day. He lived his life well and provided for a close, happy family, building up a busy career among the stone cottages of Longworth, restoring and improving many a fine home.

By now Fred and Reg were living alone - two confirmed bachelors continuing their father's business with their sister, Betty living up the road. Fred was specialising in carpentry and Reg was doing general building work. There was no shortage of jobs to do and their lives looked set fair to continue in this vein until retirement. But their lives were to change dramatically in the late 1960s.

White Lodge (Duck Cottage)

Two ladies, Mrs Antoinette Anna Lydia Skinner (known as Lydia), widow of Edward Arthur Skinner, and who had been born in the Netherlands in 1914, and her step-daughter Miss Mary Josephine Skinner born in Surrey in 1935, came to Longworth in 1969 when Mary obtained a job as caterer at the Post Office sorting office in Oxford. They bought an old stone cottage on the north side of Appleton Road – the last one at the eastern end of the village, at that time standing alone on the edge of fields except for a ruined hovel which has long since had its stones recycled, and probably buried in various walls in the village. The stone cottage that Mary and Lydia bought was called White Lodge. It had been sold to them as: 'A period house thought to be over two hundred years old, built with a roughcast finish, 'snow-cemmed' white under a tiled roof . . . in good decorative order, with double glazing and a half acre garden . . . . an unusual property which is well worth viewing.' The vendor was R. L. Edwards, the father of Colin Edwards who later married Betty Mansell's daughter Marilyn.

The Royal Oak

Despite living well outside the village both ladies were highly sociable and soon got to know a great deal about their property, not least, that it had had a change of name! They found that the cottage had been recently converted from a public house - The Royal Oak. Mary and Lydia found a board hidden away in the cottage. It read, 'Mrs Harding - Proprietor. Royal Oak'. The sign was later given to Cyril Peverill who was Mrs Harding's son by her first husband.

The Royal Oak had been known in later years as 'The Fluttering Duck', or 'The Duck' and had in fact been an 'ale-house' – a two bar pub where anyone was welcome. This 'open house' policy may have been its undoing. Mrs Harding had been the last licensee there after her husband Bill had died. Previously her husband had been licensee at the Blue Boar and they had run it together. In the 1930s the Blue Boar had the only full licence in the village centre and

A surviving china ale tankard from the Fluttering Duck.

was able to sell beer, wines and spirits, whereas the New Inn, The Crown and the Royal Oak had only a licence to sell beer. On the Faringdon Road the Lamb & Flag and the Waggon & Horses both had full licences. The Waggon & Horses was probably the oldest. At one time the Longworth landlords ran a stage waggon (a cart) to London and back with eight white horses known as the Longworth Team, carrying goods and sometimes passengers, like a long distance carrier's cart.

Many landlords of the period had secondary occupations: George Harding, landlord of the Blue Boar and then the Royal Oak, had run a small market garden; Arthur Hobbs at the New Inn had a private hire car business and did car maintenance (he later became chauffeur to Miss Raphael at Kingston House); and Harry Waterman at the Lamb & Flag ran a market garden. George Harding had married

Mrs Hilda Peverill and was stepfather to her son Cyril who had served in the Second World War as a Sergeant Major but he died well before Mary and Lydia's arrival. He is seen in the photograph of Hilda Richings' wedding to Fred Gutteridge back in 1928 (see pages 81 and 82). Mrs Harding was Fred Gutteridge's aunt. It was always a small world in Longworth! When Hilda Harding left the Royal Oak she went to live in as housekeeper to Bill Costar, at Number 3 Butts. She eventually inherited the house after his death.

White Lodge renamed Duck Cottage

Mary and Lydia decided that they would need to have White Lodge renovated it suffered from damp walls and had further water damage after six inches of water flooded the kitchen - they needed to dry out the damp-riddled walls and refurbish many of the rooms. They had architect's plans drawn up and appointed builders recommended by their new friends and neighbours in the village to carry out their wishes. They also determined to change the name of White Lodge to Duck Cottage after it was converted, as a reminder of its common name in the village, once the renovation was complete.

The builders appointed by Mary and Lydia were the firm of H. Mansell. Mary heard that Reg was considered to be a really good plasterer. He with Fred, by now a master builder, like his father before him, began a major refurbishment of the cottage. They even raised the ceilings to give more head-room to allow Lydia's big pieces of furniture to be brought in from storage. The brothers worked on the cottage for many months and became firm friends of the two ladies. But Mary and Lydia were told it was, 'no good getting to know them. They are confirmed bachelors.' Then in 1972 Reg and Fred's sister Betty Mansell sadly died, aged only 50. The two men, Fred and Reg were on their own.

Lydia said:

"Some weekends we used to go with both of them to Vintage Steam Rallies where there were also fairground organs which reminded me of my home country – Holland. We became very friendly."

The foursome did indeed become very close. Harry Mansell had met his future wife, Flo, through his building work and now Fred and Reg met their wives in similar vein - leading to a complete change in personal fortunes for the brothers – and for Lydia and Mary! On September 22nd 1973 Mary and Fred married in Longworth Church by which time Mary had left the Post Office.

Reg, Fred, Mary and Lydia. 22nd September 1973.

The marriage of Mary and Fred was witnessed by Lydia and Reg. There was some surprise that Reg and Lydia didn't get married at the same time but Lydia, always really thoughtful, said in her book of memoirs, "We did not have a double wedding as I thought it wise to wait until I was in receipt of my pension." Reg and Lydia married in 1974.

Reg, Lydia, Mary and Fred.

The house in Butts Lane was sold up but the brothers kept on a piece of land they required as a builder's yard at the top of Lodge Lane.

The two couples continued to live at the newly refurbished Duck Cottage. Young Harry Edward Reginald Mansell (named after Fred's father, Fred's brother and Mary's father) was born to a delighted Mary and Fred on 20th November 1976. He was to be the last of the line. Young Harry was born with learning difficulties but was a delightful little boy seen here with Lydia and Reg.

Young Harry is fondly remembered by many in the village. He had a wonderful childhood but it became increasingly clear that he would have to have special schooling and he would spend a great deal of time away at school.

Fred and Mary.

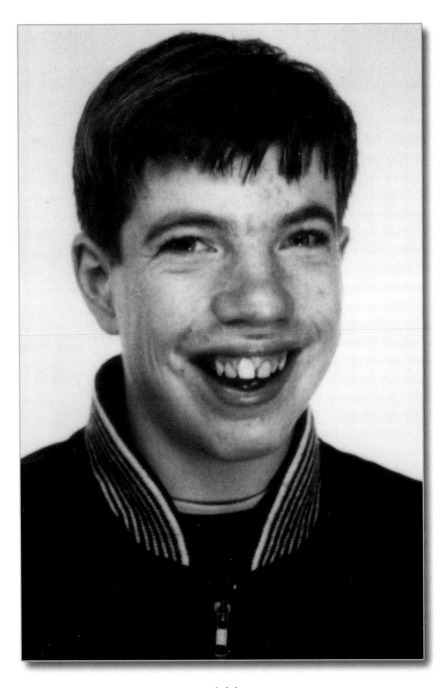

Lydia and Reg did not have many years together. On 13th May 1977 Reg died, aged 61, following a bout of angina. The remaining threesome lived on at Duck Cottage but began to make plans to build a bungalow on the land next to Fred's builder's yard at the top of Lodge Lane. With raids on many builders' yards in the county it was wise, even with retirement in prospect, to live on-hand to protect valuable equipment and supplies.

In 1985 after many years when planning permission for building their new bungalow eluded them, Fred, Mary and Lydia moved to a caravan on this plot of land, ready to build their new bungalow, and following an uncomfortable winter the bungalow, Little Owls, was ready for occupation in June 1986.

Fred retired and, with no one to take on the family business, 'H. Mansell' was wound up. The market for the small ornate stone items that Harry used to make had dropped off with the approach of war and did not pick up afterwards and so the moulds, no longer of any use, were abandoned.

Fred spent the rest of his retirement years contentedly with Mary and Lydia and young Harry when home from school. A few years later, on 12th October 1990, Fred died of Pick's disease, a form of dementia, aged 70. Lydia long outlived Reg. She died on 4th December 2008 aged 94. The family grave lies in Longworth churchyard against the east wall, not far from the Blackwell family tomb.

Left: Young Harry Mansell at about 17 to 18 years old when he returned to Longworth from school.

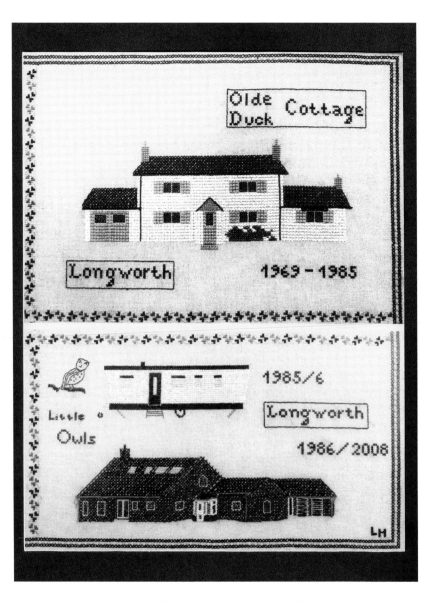

Lydia's cross stitch work.

In conclusion

Young Harry Mansell now lives happily in a home in Bedfordshire and his mother Mary has left Longworth and moved to be nearer to him.

Harry, Reg and Fred Mansell were all builders and like most of their generation never had the opportunity to choose their trade or profession but had to follow the path chosen by their father in the absence of money and knowledge of other options. Old Harry was born over a decade before the death of Queen Victoria, at a time when there were no pensions or social welfare payments and when most women did not work except in the most menial of circumstances.

Certainly Betty Mansell worked where she could - but few women of her background could at that time follow a chosen career path when they lived in a rural working class village – until the war intervened. But the whole family lived a good life, a quiet life on the whole, and despite all the suffering they left the world a much better place than they found it. Their lives were anything but ordinary.

The Mansell family represent in so many ways all of those families who lived in Longworth from the early twentieth century. Today Longworth again has no one by the name of Mansell living there – and few of the new residents will ever know that such families as the Mansells were ever there – hence this record. But Harry Mansell's life and work, and that of his and his wife Flo's family, touched so many other lives during their time in the village. The work of Harry, Reg and Fred Mansell will endure until other builders come and refurbish yet again all those lovely old stone cottages in and around Longworth.

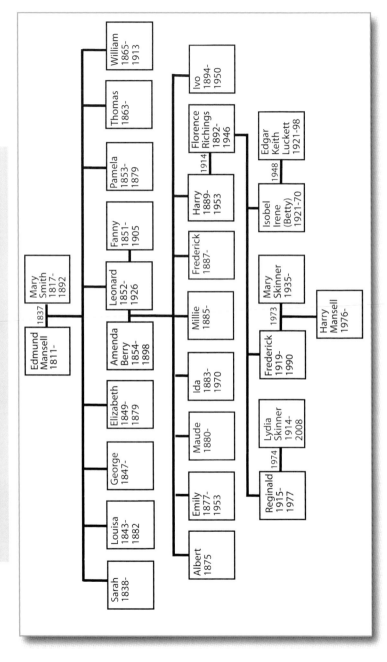

Mansell Family Tree

Edmund Mansell 1811– —1837— Mary Smith 1817–1892

Children: Sarah 1838–, Louisa 1843–1882, George 1847–, Elizabeth 1849–1879, Leonard 1852–1926, Fanny 1851–1905, Pamela 1853–1879, Thomas 1863–, William 1865–1913

Leonard 1852–1926 & Amenda Berry 1854–1898

Children: Albert 1875, Emily 1877–1953, Maude 1880, Ida 1883–1970, Millie 1885–, Frederick 1887–, Harry 1889–1953 —1914— Florence Richings 1892–1946, Ivo 1894–1950

Frederick 1919–1990 —1973— Mary Skinner 1935–

Harry Mansell 1976–

Reginald 1915–1977 —1974— Lydia Skinner 1914–2008

Isobel Irene (Betty) 1921–70 —1948— Edgar Keith Luckett 1921–98

Richings Family Tree

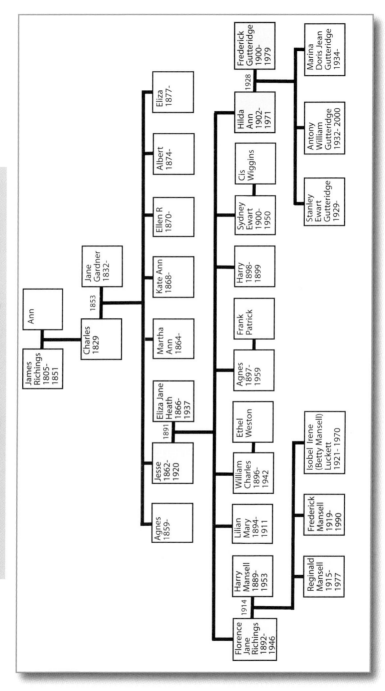

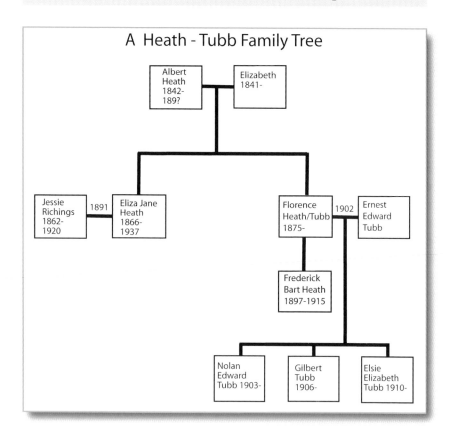

A Heath - Tubb Family Tree

Albert Heath 1842-189?

Elizabeth 1841-

Jessie Richings 1862-1920

1891

Eliza Jane Heath 1866-1937

Florence Heath/Tubb 1875-

1902

Ernest Edward Tubb

Frederick Bart Heath 1897-1915

Nolan Edward Tubb 1903-

Gilbert Tubb 1906-

Elsie Elizabeth Tubb 1910-

Acknowledgements

Especial thanks to Mary Mansell and also to Stan Gutteridge, and his late brother Tony, who have been a major source of photographs and information over many years; to Nigel Drew for his remarkable emails and for reviewing the script and to Rob Belk and Quentin Drew for their helpful suggestions; to Iris Graham for information; and to Marilyn Edwards (née Luckett) for the loan of embroidered postcards.

I owe a large debt of gratitude to my editor Peter Keene - Longworth and District History Society Publications' Officer who has published this book. Thanks also to Janet Keene for proof-reading and for her everlasting patience.

Longworth & District History Society is grateful for the generous donation from Mary Mansell and for the grant from the Hinton and Longworth Educational Fund (HALF) towards the cost of production.

Jan Kelly. April 2013.

Illustrations Index

Illustrations - index

Illustrations - index

Further Reading on Longworth

Longworth Rose is the 12-page (A4) magazine of Longworth and District History Society and is published three times a year.
Volume 1 (1998 - 2005) consists of the first 24 issues, also bound into a 292-page book. ISBN 978-0948444-45-6.
Volume 2 (2006-2013), the next 24 issues. Issue Vol (2), No 24 (September 2013) includes an additional comprehensive index to all articles in both volumes, listing many Longworth related references. The bound version of Volume Two is ISBN 978-0-948444-62-3.

Longworth Through the Centuries by Jasmine S. Howse. This is a combined facsimile edition (2007) of twin books first published in 1980 and 1982. 163 pages, plus appendix and 33 illustrations. A comprehensively researched book. Chapter headings include: Early period, Medieval period, Sixteenth century, Seventeenth century, Eighteenth century, Nineteenth century. ISBN 978-0948444-51-7

Longworth – a Sense of Place edited by Peter Keene with Janet Keene and Jan Kelly (2000). 64 pages (A5). 34 illustrations. The booklet is best described as a combined village companion, guided walk and reference book. The emphasis is upon the way life in the village has been transformed during the past hundred years. ISBN 978-0-948444-40-1.

Growing up in Longworth by Ray Dunsdon (2010).
123 pages (A4). 60 black and white illustrations. Ray Dunsdon marshalls his recollections of childhood and adolescence in Longworth which was, at that time, a small, almost self-sufficient, Berkshire village. The resulting book recalls, with candour and humour, the harsh life of the times, including the idiosyncrasies of its inhabitants as seen through the eyes of a teenager. A sharply focussed record of village life over half a century ago. ISBN 978-0-948444-54-8 (2010).

Prince's Roses; a hundred years of Longworth Roses by Jan Kelly. 96 pages (A5). 90 illustrations. With meticulous research Jan Kelly has documented the remarkable growth, and eventual decline, of the rose industry in Longworth. Principally the result of the entrepreneurial drive of two families - the Princes and the Drews. The Longworth rose industry grew rapidly in the late 19th and early 20th century, gaining an international reputation and winning numerous awards throughout the U K. ISBN 978-0948444-53-1 (2009)

For more about Longworth and District History Society, its activities and publications see **www.l-h-s.org.uk**

Publications of Longworth and District History Society
(Longworth, Kingston Bagpuize, Southmoor, Hinton Waldrist)

Longworth Rambler. Free pamphlet of LHS programme & contacts.

Longworth Rose. Magazine of Longworth & District History Society. For full content details of Vol. One & Two visit **www.l-h-s.org.uk**

Growing up in Longworth by Ray Dunsdon (2010). 123 pages (A4). 60 black and white illustrations.

Prince's Roses; a hundred years of Longworth Roses by Jan Kelly. (2009) 96 pages (A5). 90 illustrations.

Longworth, a sense of place (2000). A combined guided walk, village companion and reference book. 64 pages (A5). 34 illust.

Longworth Through the Centuries by Jasmine S. Howse. A facsimile edition (2007) of two books first published 1980-82. 163 pages (A5). Plus appendix. 33 illustrations.

Kingston Bagpuize with Southmoor, a sense of place. (2001). A combined guided walk, village companion and reference book. 72 pages (A5). 44 illustrations.

The Life and Times of Southmoor Methodist Chapel (2007) by Jan Kelly. A history of the chapel and of the families intimately connected with it. 76 pages (A4). 75 illustrations.

Village Millennium, a history of Kingston Bagpuize and Southmoor by W.R. Carmichael. 36 pages (A5). 9 illustrations. (1971). Reprinted in 2007 as a facsimile edition.

The Cultivators by Murray Maclean (1970). Brief history of the agriculture in Kingston Bagpuize & Southmoor. 16 Pages (A5). 12 illustrations. Facsimile edition with update (2007).

Letter to Pippa by Sybil Beard (1998). 110 pages (A5). 18 photos. An evocation of life between the wars in Kingston Bagpuize.

Dawn to Dusk; reminiscences of a wonderful life by Graham A. Platt (2012). 128 pages (A5). 40 Illustrations.

Hinton Waldrist, a sense of place. (2000). A combined guided walk, village companion & reference book. 56 pages (A5). 46 illust.

Hinton Waldrist Through the Centuries by Jasmine Howse. A 2007 facsimile edition of a book first published in two parts in 1968 &1969. 166 pages (A5). 23 illustrations. Combines parts 1 & 2.

Oxfordshire Countryside - five circular walks by Peter & Janet Keene (2003). Walks in the Longworth, Hinton Waldrist & KBS area. 60 pages (A4) In plastic folder + pocket-size guide map for all walks.

Published for Longworth and District History Society by Thematic Trails. 7 Norwood Avenue, Kingston Bagpuize, Oxfordshire OX13 5AD.
Catalogue and online ordering: **www.thematic-trails.org**
Tel:01865-820522   Email: keene@thematic-trails.org

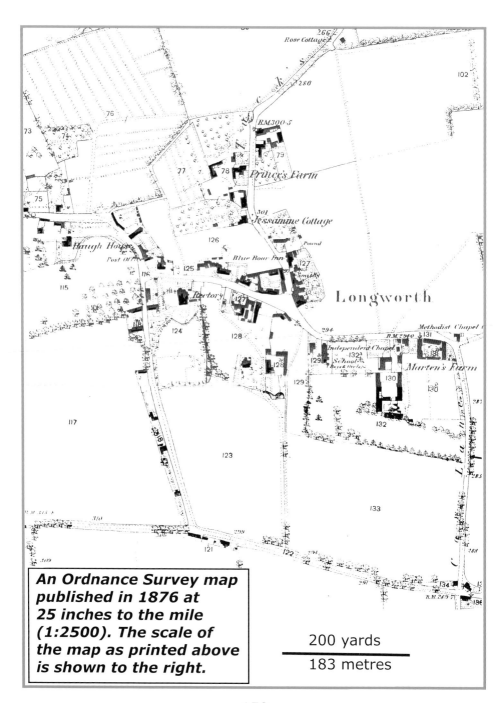

An Ordnance Survey map published in 1876 at 25 inches to the mile (1:2500). The scale of the map as printed above is shown to the right.

200 yards

183 metres

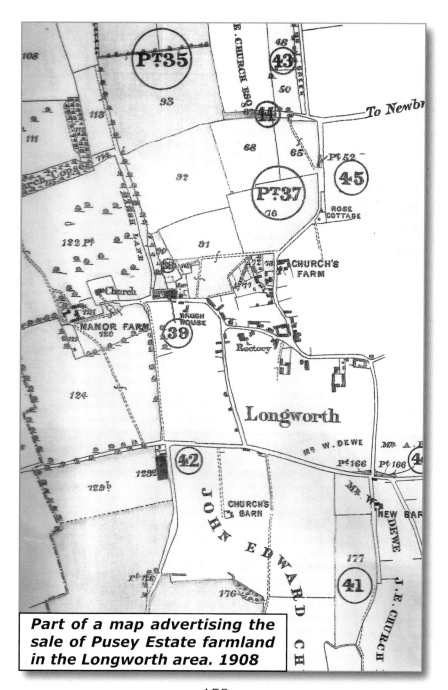

Part of a map advertising the sale of Pusey Estate farmland in the Longworth area. 1908

St Mary's Church and Manor, Longworth from the west.